CONTEMPORARY ISSUES COMPANION

| Eu

D1070367

Other Books of Related Interest:

Opposing Viewpoints Series

Abortion

Death and Dying

The Death Penalty

Euthanasia

Homosexuality

Problems of Death

Suicide

Teens at Risk

Current Controversies Series

The Abortion Controversy

Assisted Suicide

Capital Punishment

Medical Ethics

Mental Health

Suicide

At Issue Series

Anitdepressants

The Ethics of Abortion

The Ethics of Capital Punishment

The Ethics of Euthanasia

How Should One Cope with Death?

Physician-Assisted Suicide

The Right to Die

Euthanasia

Sylvia Engdahl, Book Editor

GREENHAVEN PRESS

An imprint of Thomson Gale, a part of The Thomson Corporation

Detroit • New York • San Francisco • New Haven, Conn. • Waterville, Maine • London

Christine Nasso, *Publisher*
Elizabeth Des Chenes, *Managing Editor*

© 2007 Thomson Gale, a part of The Thomson Corporation.

Thomson and Star logo are trademarks and Gale and Greenhaven Press are registered trademarks used herein under license.

For more information, contact:
Greenhaven Press
27500 Drake Rd.
Farmington Hills, MI 48331-3535
Or you can visit our Internet site at http://www.gale.com

Articles in Greenhaven Press anthologies are often edited for length to meet page require-ments. In addition, original titles of these works are changed to clearly present the main thesis and to explicitly indicate the author's opinion. Every effort is made to ensure that Greenhaven Press accurately reflects the original intent of the authors. Every effort has been made to trace the owners of copyrighted material.

Cover photograph reproduced by permission of iStockphoto.com/Kathy Reesey.

LIBRARY OF CONGRESS CATALOGING-IN-PUBLICATION DATA

Euthanasia / Sylvia Engdahl, book editor.
    p. cm. -- (Contemporary issues companion)
  Includes bibliographical references and index.
  ISBN-13: 978-0-7377-3251-1 (hardcover : alk. paper)
  ISBN-10: 0-7377-3251-2 (hardcover : alk. paper)
  ISBN-13: 978-0-7377-3252-8 (pbk. : alk. paper)
  ISBN-10: 0-7377-3252-0 (pbk. : alk. paper)
  1. Euthanasia--Moral and ethical aspects--Juvenile literature. 2. Assisted suicide--Moral and ethical aspects--Juvenile literature. I. Engdahl, Sylvia Louise.
  R726E783 2007
  179.7--dc22
                                                        2006022933

Printed in the United States of America
10 9 8 7 6 5 4 3 2 1

Contents

Foreword

In the news, on the streets, and in neighborhoods, individuals are confronted with a variety of social problems. Such problems may affect people directly: A young woman may struggle with depression, suspect a friend of having bulimia, or watch a loved one battle cancer. And even the issues that do not directly affect her private life—such as religious cults, domestic violence, or legalized gambling—still impact the larger society in which she lives. Discovering and analyzing the complexities of issues that encompass communal and societal realms as well as the world of personal experience is a valuable educational goal in the modern world.

Effectively addressing social problems requires familiarity with a constantly changing stream of data. Becoming well informed about today's controversies is an intricate process that often involves reading myriad primary and secondary sources, analyzing political debates, weighing various experts' opinions—even listening to firsthand accounts of those directly affected by the issue. For students and general observers, this can be a daunting task because of the sheer volume of information available in books, periodicals, on the evening news, and on the Internet. Researching the consequences of legalized gambling, for example, might entail sifting through congressional testimony on gambling's societal effects, examining private studies on Indian gaming, perusing numerous websites devoted to Internet betting, and reading essays written by lottery winners as well as interviews with recovering compulsive gamblers. Obtaining valuable information can be time-consuming—since it often requires researchers to pore over numerous documents and commentaries before discovering a source relevant to their particular investigation.

Greenhaven's Contemporary Issues Companion series seeks to assist this process of research by providing readers with useful and pertinent information about today's complex issues. Each volume in this anthology series focuses on a topic of current interest, presenting informative and thought-provoking selections written from a wide variety of viewpoints. The readings selected by the editors include such diverse sources as personal accounts and case studies, pertinent factual and statistical articles, and relevant commentaries and over views. This diversity of sources and views, found in every Contemporary Issues Companion, offers readers a broad perspective in one convenient volume.

In addition, each title in the Contemporary Issues Companion series is designed especially for young adults. The selections included in every volume are chosen for their accessibility and are expertly edited in consideration of both the reading and comprehension levels of the audience. The structure of the anthologies also enhances accessibility. An introductory essay places each issue in context and provides helpful facts such as historical background or current statistics and legislation that pertain to the topic. The chapters that follow organize the material and focus on specific aspects of the book's topic. Every essay is introduced by a brief summary of its main points and biographical information about the author. These summaries aid in comprehension and can also serve to direct readers to material of immediate interest and need. Finally, a comprehensive index allows readers to efficiently scan and locate content.

The Contemporary Issues Companion series is an ideal launching point for research on a particular topic. Each anthology in the series is composed of readings taken from an extensive gamut of resources, including periodicals, newspapers, books, government documents, the publications of private and public organizations, and Internet websites. In these volumes, readers will find factual support suitable for use in reports, debates, speeches, and research papers. The anthologies also facilitate further research, featuring a book and periodical bibliography and a list of organizations to contact for additional information.

A perfect resource for both students and the general reader, Greenhaven's Contemporary Issues Companion series is sure to be a valued source of current, readable information on social problems that interest young adults. It is the editors' hope that readers will find the Contemporary Issues Companion series useful as a starting point to formulate their own opinions about and answers to the complex issues of the present day.

Introduction

Euthanasia, which comes from the Greek words for "easy death," has traditionally meant killing, or permitting the death, of incurably sick individuals for reasons of mercy. Today the term usually has a narrower meaning. At present most writers use the term *euthanasia* only when referring to what used to be called *active euthanasia*—an action by someone such as a doctor that directly causes death (for example, the administration of a lethal injection). In contrast, when a doctor merely prescribes a lethal dose of medication for a terminally ill patient to take without help, the death is referred to as *physician-assisted suicide*. While the former practice is illegal in the United States and most other nations, the latter is presently the subject of controversy. Oregon is currently the only U.S. state that permits assisted suicide, and its law—which became effective in 1997—is often the center of debate.

A related controversy in health care today is the withholding or withdrawal of life-sustaining medical treatment in order to allow a patient to die naturally. Some opponents of this practice consider it *passive euthanasia*, but that term is no longer widely used in such cases. To refuse medical treatment is the legal right of any adult who is conscious and mentally competent. That this right extends to the refusal of life-sustaining treatment was confirmed by the New Jersey Supreme Court in the 1976 case of Karen Quinlan and by the U.S. Supreme Court in the 1990 case of Nancy Cruzan. When a patient is unconscious, withdrawal of treatment—especially artificial nutrition and hydration—remains controversial, although a surrogate can legally refuse treatment if the patient had previously made his or her wishes clear. Even in debate about it, however, this is generally viewed as an issue separate from euthanasia and physician-assisted suicide.

Another contentious phrase in the controversies surrounding end-of-life issues is *right to die*. Before the right to refuse life-sustaining treatment was legally established, doctors and hospitals sometimes kept suffering patients alive against their will or kept unconscious patients on long-term life support against the wishes of their families. People who objected to this practice formed "right to die" organizations to work for change. Since this right is now recognized by the courts, the meaning of "right to die" has shifted, and now it usually refers to advocacy of assisted suicide. A related term sometimes applied to assisted suicide by its proponents is *death with dignity*. For example, Oregon's assisted-suicide law is titled the Death with Dignity Act.

Although euthanasia in the narrow sense is against the law throughout the United States, it is legal in the Netherlands and Belgium. Many people believe that legalizing physician-assisted suicide inevitably leads to a demand for euthanasia. Some fear that *voluntary euthanasia* at the request of patients would be supplemented by *non-voluntary euthanasia*, the active killing of incompetent patients, and eventually even *involuntary euthanasia*, the killing of competent patients who have not requested it. Surveys in the Netherlands have shown that involuntary euthanasia has already occurred. On the other hand, some proponents of euthanasia argue that prohibition of active euthanasia is too restrictive. It is discrimination, they say, to deny people who are physically incapable of taking medication themselves the option of ending their lives.

In the past few years there has been more widespread controversy about these issues than there was even a decade ago. This is partly because the legalization of assisted suicide in Oregon and attempts to pass similar laws in other states have aroused heated opposition on the part of religious, pro-life, and disability rights groups. It is also due to growing worry that an aging population and rising medical costs may lead to a social climate in which hastening the death of terminally ill patients is seen as normal. A common fear is that the right to die will gradually turn into a perceived duty to die. Availability of the option might encourage people to choose death simply to avoid becoming a burden on their families or on society. Disability rights organizations have expressed concern over the possibility that if the deliberate ending of life becomes acceptable, the public will view the lives of disabled persons as not worth living. Some of the ill and elderly have the same concern. Others believe, however, that if a time comes when they prefer death to living in a way they find intolerable, they should not be prevented by the government from receiving assistance in dying quickly and painlessly.

The largest increase in awareness of end-of-life issues occurred in 2005–2006 when three highly-publicized events brought these issues into the spotlight. First, the movie *Million Dollar Baby* won four Academy Awards. That movie dealt in part with an injured woman boxer's wish to die rather than remain on life support. Her decision and her coach's decision to help her die aroused controversy (the fact that she would have had the legal right to refuse further medical treatment was ignored). Then, a much larger controversy arose over the case of Terri Schiavo, a Florida woman who was in a persistent vegetative state due to an injury. Her husband had asked that treatment be terminated. Schiavo's parents and family, however, disputed the husband's right to decide and a long legal contest ensued—involving not only the courts, legislature, and governor of Florida, but the U.S. Congress and even the president. Encouraged by ongoing media coverage, the public took sides in the bitter debate over whether she should be kept alive. In 2005, after more than a decade, the court ordered Schiavo's feeding tube removed in accordance with her husband's instructions. She died in a way that some people envisioned as horrifying and others viewed as natural.

The third event to attract national notice was the Supreme Court's consideration of whether the federal government could take action against Oregon doctors who participate in assisted suicides. This case was not about the legality of assisted suicide itself; the only point at issue was the applicability of the federal Controlled Substances Act—which is aimed at drug dealers—to the prescription of lethal drugs. The Court ruled that no legal action could be undertaken via that act because lethal prescriptions serve a medical purpose under Oregon law. Headlines announced that the Court had "upheld" Oregon's law, to the relief of supporters and the dismay of opponents who had campaigned heavily against it. Both sides now say the decision may lead to attempts to pass assisted suicide laws in other states. However, quite a few such attempts have failed since Oregon's law was passed; and although polls show that in principle, a majority of Americans favor allowing terminally ill individuals to end their lives at their discretion, when it comes to legislation there is more controversy. Many people, after considering the potential social consequences of legalizing assisted suicide, have second thoughts.

Until recently, comparatively few people talked about assisted death unless they were strongly in favor of it. Now that it has become a well-publicized and sensitive political issue, proponents of assisted death are less vocal than they once were. Several major advocacy organizations, including the formerly-prominent Hemlock Society, have disbanded and have been replaced by groups that emphasize palliative care, that is, treatment that provides physical and psychological comfort for the dying—a service everyone agrees should be expanded. "People's worst nightmare is that powerful politicians will rob them of a peaceful death," said Barbara Coombs Lee, head of Compassion and Choices, a group that includes hastened death among the choices it supports. This is unquestionably true, but the concept of a peaceful death differs from person to person, and there are also people who fear that they, or others who are vulnerable, may be robbed of their last months of life.

CHAPTER 1

Assisted Death in Current Practice

Public Opinion Is Divided on End-of-Life Issues

Public Agenda

Public Agenda is a nonpartisan, nonprofit organization that researches public opinion and prepares reports on current issues. The following selection is its 2006 summary of public attitudes toward end-of-life issues for the terminally ill. Public opinion is sharply divided on these issues. Some people believe euthanasia and physician-assisted suicide would simply acknowledge their right to decide when and how they will die. Others fear legalizing assisted death would lead to neglect of the old, the poor, and the disabled, or that the right to die might become a duty to die when medical care became too costly. Still others have religious or moral objections. Public Agenda notes that court rulings have done little to resolve these concerns. The organization does conclude that the public does seem to feel strongly that decisions about whether to keep permanently-unconscious patients on life support are best made by families and doctors, not the government.

Dying, for most Americans, has become far more complicated than it once was. A century ago, most people died at home of illnesses that medicine could do little to defeat. Now technology has created choices for dying patients and their families, choices that raise basic questions about human dignity and what constitutes a "good death."

Most people die in hospitals or institutions where the staff makes a valiant effort to keep patients alive until there is no reasonable chance of recovery. For many people, that's exactly what they want: a no-holds-barred effort to fight off death as long as possible. For others facing terminal illness, however, there may come a point where the fight no longer seems worth it. Those patients may find their wishes and those of their families overlooked as physicians juggle medical, legal and moral considerations. In most cases, medical professionals have considerable discretion in deciding when additional efforts to sustain life are futile and a patient should be allowed to die.

Court rulings have firmly established a patient's legal right to discontinue life-sustaining treatment, such as respirators or artificial nutrition. There's also extensive precedent for allowing family members to decide whether to continue treatment or end feeding when an incapacitated patient is no longer able to decide for themselves—but as the Terri Schiavo case showed, even that debate is not settled. What is also unresolved is whether individuals should be able to ask physicians to hasten their deaths and whether it is morally acceptable for physicians to do so.

Fundamental Questions

The debate over "end-of-life issues" raises fundamental questions:

Who decides whether a life is worth living or not? Many people say they would rather die than suffer in great pain, or be trapped in a vegetative state. Should people have the right to decide when and how they will die? Should others—their families, their doctors, the government—be able to decide for them?

Is euthanasia—the supposedly merciful killing of the terminally ill—an act of kindness prompted by a sense of mercy and respect for an individual's wishes? Or is it an act of murder and a violation of the Hippocratic oath?

If legally recognized, would physician-assisted suicide permit dying people a measure of control over the timing and manner of their death? Or would it lead to a slippery slope of neglect for the old, the poor, the disabled and those who are emotionally distraught or seriously ill? Would the right to die become the duty to die when living would be too costly for patients and their survivors?

What are the religious and moral questions here? For people in many faiths, these decisions touch on their most deeply held belief that life and death should be left to God, not human beings. Others argue that life is to be cherished and not abandoned, no matter the circumstances.

Are there other alternatives? Advocates of palliative care say the real problem is that terminal patients don't get enough pain relief and emotional support. Many of the terminally ill suffer from treatable clinical depression. Others get less pain relief than they should because doctors are reluctant to use painkillers aggressively enough. Over the last few decades, a network of hospices have grown up specifically to make terminal patients as comfortable as possible in their last months.

Ballot Initiatives and Court Decisions

Although it is widely condoned around the world, only . . . the Netherlands [and Belgium have] made physician-assisted suicide legal. In the United States, voters in five states initiated ballot measures to legalize it. All have failed, except for Oregon, where voters in 1994 approved the "Death with Dignity Act." That measure permits doctors to prescribe a lethal drug dose but not administer it and established rules to ensure patients seeking assisted suicide are mentally competent, in great pain and intent on ending their lives. Since the law took effect in 1997, more than 200 people have committed suicide with the aid of a physician, according to the Oregon Department of Human Services.

[In 2006], the U.S. Supreme Court has . . . [decided] whether the federal government can block the Oregon law. The Bush administration argue[d] that the federal government has jurisdiction over prescription medicine, and that Oregon's law violated federal controlled-substance laws. A federal district judge rejected the suit, saying the Justice Department has no standing to decide "what constitutes the legitimate practice of medicine," and also claimed the attorney general was attempting to "stifle an ongoing, earnest and profound debate in the various states concerning physician-assisted suicide." [The Supreme Court ruling upheld the district judge.]

But the Supreme Court, in two unanimous 1997 decisions, ... upheld assisted-suicide bans in New York and Washington state, saying terminally ill patients have no legal right to medical help in committing suicide. In Michigan, Dr. Jack Kevorkian, who has publicly acknowledged helping 130 people commit suicide, was convicted of second-degree murder in 1999 and sentenced to 10 to 25 years in prison for administering a fatal injection to a terminally ill man.

Those rulings have done little to resolve murky and practical concerns that many Americans have about how they will die. While ruling that states may ban the practice, the high court suggested that the issue is not yet resolved. Chief Justice William Rehnquist wrote that the court's decision "permits this debate to continue, as it should in a democratic society."

Physician's Dilemma

Physicians continue to face a pointed dilemma. "For over 2,000 years, the predominant responsibility of the physician has not been to preserve life at all costs but to serve the patient's needs while respecting the patient's autonomy and dignity," the American Medical Association [AMA] said in one legal brief. But the AMA opposes physician-assisted suicide. The Hippocratic oath still states: "To please no one will I prescribe a deadly drug, or give advice which may cause his death."

A poll taken among Oregon physicians provides one indication of the dilemma: While 60 percent say physician-assisted suicide should be legal, only 46 percent said they would be willing to prescribe lethal medicine.

For the vast majority of people, assisted suicide is not a legal option—and even if it was, large numbers say they wouldn't consider it. For most, the question is how long to maintain treatment. Every state now allows people to issue some form of advance directive, "living will" or health care proxy to specify what course of action they want their physicians to pursue if they're unable to communicate.

But living wills are limited in their effect. For a start, only about four in 10 Americans have advance directives. They're not always binding. And many physicians are unaware of their patients' wishes, or unwilling to implement them. Realistically, if an advance directive hasn't been discussed and agreed to by family members and doctors, it may not carry much weight.

The Terri Schiavo case, which riveted the nation for weeks in 2005, demonstrated the worst-case scenario in an end-of-life situation: a brain-damaged patient without a written advance directive, a family bitterly divided on what to do, years of litigation and heavy pressure from politicians and advocacy groups. The courts consistently ruled in favor of Schiavo's husband, who eventually won the right to remove her feeding tube over her parents' objections. One consequence of the case was a surge of public interest in living wills. Another is that some 20 states have introduced bills to clarify existing laws on advance directives and guardianship for the incapacitated.

Conflicted Public

This is an intensely personal issue for the public. Surveys show about one-third of Americans say they've had to decide whether to keep a loved one alive using extraordinary means. Polls also show that over the past half century, the percentage of Americans who say that doctors should be allowed to help end an incurably ill patient's life painlessly when the patient and the patient's family request it has doubled to about 70 percent.

But when the question is posed in less abstract terms—such as modifying the question to include the phrase "assisted suicide" —support dwindles, and supporters only slightly outnumber opponents. There also seems to be a distinction in the public's mind between what they would choose for themselves and what they would choose for others, with far fewer saying they would choose to end treatment for a spouse or child than for themselves. People are divided on whether they would help a terminally ill relative or friend commit suicide to end their suffering.

The public does seem to feel strongly that these are decisions best made by families and doctors, not the government, and most disapproved of Congress' effort to intervene in the Schiavo case.

It Is Legal for Conscious, Rational Patients to Refuse Medical Life Support

James J. Murtagh

James J. Murtagh has spent more than twenty years as an intensive care unit physician and is a former associate professor of internal medicine at Emory University. In the following selection he points out that the movie Million Dollar Baby, *which won the 2005 Academy Award for Best Picture, is misleading because it ignores the fact that conscious, mentally competent patients can reject any medical care they do not want, including life-sustaining care. In the movie, the heroine is shown as fully conscious and completely rational. Therefore, Murtagh explains, the law would have required doctors to turn off her respirator if she asked them to—she would not have had to persuade a friend to do it. This right was confirmed by the 1976 case of Karen Quinlan when the New Jersey Supreme Court ruled that due to the right to privacy, patients (or if unconscious, their families) have the right to refuse treatment, even if doing so results in death.*

When they open the envelope for [2004] "Best Picture" at the Oscars tonight, I'll be rooting hard for *Million Dollar Baby*—the dazzling new Clint Eastwood film about a woman left paralyzed after sustaining a neck injury during a boxing match.

Because I like the movie so much, it's no fun to report that both the film and its critics have made a major mistake: they forgot that it's illegal for doctors to treat alert, rational patients against their will. Somehow, the film distorts the medical aspects of end-of-life decision-making almost beyond recognition.

James J. Murtagh, "Movie-Inspired Debate over 'Euthanasia' Is Absurd," *Dissident Voice*, February 27, 2005. Reproduced by permission of the author and *Dissident Voice*, www.dissidentvoice.org.

Indeed, the movie's depiction of Hilary Swank's character (the Baby) as paralyzed on a ventilator and begging a friend to "pull the plug"—by sneaking into the hospital, turning off her respirator and giving her a shot of adrenaline—completely ignores the reality of routine medical ethics. Where was the patient's doctor? That doctor had a moral, legal and religious duty to honor the patient's wishes!

Failure to Honor Patient's Wishes Is Illegal

No one has to guess what Swank wants. She's not unconscious, she's not a vegetable, she's not depressed. She's depicted as completely rational. Which means that her wishes must be obeyed. As a matter of fact, failing to honor a patient's instructions for these end-of-life procedures is actually illegal—and theoretically could result in criminal prosecution of any doctor who insisted on keeping a patient alive artificially against the patient's will.

Unfortunately, the medical premise of *Million Dollar Baby* is dead wrong, because Baby could have refused the ventilator without a quibble, merely by asking. Since the famous Karen Quinlan case 30 years ago, U.S. doctors have been totally prohibited from insisting on unwanted therapy against a patient's wishes.

Pope Pius XII, himself, understood as much in 1952, when he condemned "extraordinary means" to maintain life against the will of patients. The major religions are in agreement. I have worked with chaplains and rabbis of all faiths to help patients make these decisions—and most of the priests I work with have written advanced directives to ensure they are never placed on a ventilator against their will.

Gray areas do arise when a patient is unconscious, however. Difficult ethical cases come up all the time. But a rational, talking patient could have refused the ventilator, the IV fluids, medicines, surgery—or a dozen other treatments needed to stay alive. Is the film really suggesting the doctors took the patient to surgery to remove a leg, in order to save her life without her consent? Had Baby refused the operation, she would have died from infection, and she would have spared the Eastwood character his torment, and her own attempt to end her life by biting her tongue.

Apparently unaware of this medical reality, the creators of Baby came up with a thoroughly Orwellian and barbaric plot twist in order to solve a non-existent problem—by having Eastwood sneak into Baby's hospital room to pull the plug.

Debates About the Movie Ignored Key Fact

But if the movie's depiction of a typical ventilator scenario was absurdly unrealistic, the talk show and op-ed page debates that have followed it seem even more ludicrous. While conservatives Rush Limbaugh and Michael Medved huff and puff about "the sacred right to preserve life" and disability activists protest the depiction of Baby, nobody seems to have grasped a key fact: This is a total non-issue in American hospitals today!

Like most ICU doctors, I learned a great deal about end-of-life decisions during 20 years of caring for people. I do my best to treat pain and depression in these patients, while also doing everything I can to show them that life can be worth living. More than once over the years, I found myself referring to the inspiring example set by paralyzed actor Christopher Reeve, who lived a rich and creative life on a ventilator, while also becoming a hero to millions. Like Reeve, severely disabled scientist Stephen Hawking and scores of other disabled Americans are honored precisely because they've made the decision to soldier on, despite pain and obstacles.

Nonetheless, disabled patients—like all other patients—enjoy the right to refuse therapy. Jehovah's Witnesses are permitted to refuse life-saving blood, and all patients are free to refuse life-saving surgery. To insist otherwise would be to transform the ICU unit into Orwell's "Big Brother"—a tyrant who would ride roughshod over a patient's innate right to allow nature to take its course, and to die in dignity.

Like most people, I sometimes found myself wondering during my earlier years: What would happen if I became severely disabled? Would I choose to turn the ventilator off? And then it actually did happen, several years ago. Suddenly I faced the same questions that had confronted Reeve and many other disabled patients. Fortunately, I recovered, but I will never forget walking in the shoes of a critically ill patient. . . .

I am very afraid that patients seeing this film will be misled on their real options, and will wind up fearing Frankenstein ventilators run amok. As both doctor and patient, I urge all of us to ignore the medical distortions contained in this film—and to treat it as an opportunity to explore the deep and searching questions that will face us at the end of life.

Physician-Assisted Suicide Remains Low in Oregon

Oregon Department of Human Services

The Oregon Department of Human Services publishes an annual report presenting statistics on the use of the Death with Dignity Act (DWDA) for physician-assisted suicide (PAS) in Oregon. The following selection is taken from its 2006 report. The statistics show that the use of PAS is low and has remained relatively stable since 2002. The end-of-life concerns most frequently expressed by patients requesting lethal prescriptions were a decreased ability to participate in activities that make life enjoyable, loss of dignity, and concern about losing autonomy. The Human Services department states that the percentage of patients referred to a specialist for psychological evaluation has declined significantly since 1998.

The Oregon Death with Dignity Act was a citizen's initiative first passed by Oregon voters in November 1994 with 51% in favor.... In November 1997, a measure asking Oregon voters to repeal the Death with Dignity Act was placed on the general election ballot.... Voters rejected this measure by a margin of 60% to 40%, retaining the Death with Dignity Act.

Although physician-assisted suicide has been legal in Oregon for eight years, it remains highly controversial. On November 6, 2001, U.S. Attorney General John Ashcroft issued a new interpretation of the Controlled Substances Act, which would prohibit doctors from prescribing controlled substances for use in physician-assisted suicide. To date, all the medications prescribed under the Act have been barbiturates, which are controlled substances and, therefore, would be prohibited

Oregon Department of Human Services, "Excerpts," *Eighth Annual Report on Oregon's Human Dignity Act*, March 9, 2006, pp. 6, 7, 8, 11, 12, 14, 15, 16.

by this ruling for use in PAS. In response to a lawsuit filed by the State of Oregon on November 20, 2001, a U.S. district court issued a temporary restraining order against Ashcroft's ruling pending a new hearing. On April 17, 2002, U.S. District Court Judge Robert Jones upheld the Death with Dignity Act. On September 23, 2002, Attorney General Ashcroft filed an appeal, asking the Ninth U.S. Circuit Court of Appeals to overturn the District Court's ruling. The appeal was denied. . . . Ashcroft asked the U.S. Supreme Court to review the Ninth Circuit's decision. On October 5, 2005, the Supreme Court heard arguments in the case, and on January 17, 2006 it affirmed the lower court's decision. . . .

Requirements

The Death with Dignity Act allows terminally ill Oregon residents to obtain and use prescriptions from their physicians for self-administered, lethal medications. Under the Act, ending one's life in accordance with the law does not constitute suicide. However, we use "physician-assisted suicide" because that terminology is used in medical literature to describe ending life through the voluntary self-administration of lethal medications prescribed by a physician for that purpose. The Death with Dignity Act legalizes PAS, but specifically prohibits euthanasia, where a physician or other person directly administers a medication to end another's life.

To request a prescription for lethal medications, the Death with Dignity Act requires that a patient must be:

- An adult (18 years of age or older),

- A resident of Oregon,

- Capable (defined as able to make and communicate health care decisions), and

- Diagnosed with a terminal illness that will lead to death within six months.

Patients meeting these requirements are eligible to request a prescription for lethal medication from a licensed Oregon physician. To receive a prescription for lethal medication, the following steps must be fulfilled:

- The patient must make two oral requests to his or her physician, separated by at least 15 days.

- The patient must provide a written request to his or her physician, signed in the presence of two witnesses.

- The prescribing physician and a consulting physician must confirm the diagnosis and prognosis.

- The prescribing physician and a consulting physician must determine whether the patient is capable.

- If either physician believes the patient's judgment is impaired by a psychiatric or psychological disorder, the patient must be referred for a psychological examination.

- The prescribing physician must inform the patient of feasible alternatives to assisted suicide, including comfort care, hospice care, and pain control.

- The prescribing physician must request, but may not require, the patient to notify his or her next-of-kin of the prescription request. . . .

The Oregon Revised Statutes specify that action taken in accordance with the Death with Dignity Act does not constitute suicide, mercy killing or homicide under the law. . . .

Number of Patients

Both the number of prescriptions written and the number of Oregonians using PAS vary annually but have been relatively stable since 2002. In 2005, 39 physicians wrote 64 prescriptions for lethal doses of medication. In 1998, 24 prescriptions were written, followed by 33 in 1999, 39 in 2000, 44 in 2001, 58 in 2002, 68 in 2003, and 60 in 2004.

Thirty-two of the 2005 prescription recipients died after ingesting the medication. Of the 32 recipients who did not ingest the prescribed medication in 2005, 15 died from their illnesses, and 17 were alive on December 31, 2005. In addition, six patients who received prescriptions during 2004 died in 2005 as a result of ingesting their medication, giving a total of 38 PAS deaths during 2005.

In 1998, 16 Oregonians used PAS, followed by 27 in 1999, 27 in 2000, 21 in 2001, 38 in 2002, 42 in 2003, and 37 in 2004. Ratios of PAS deaths to total deaths have shown a similar trend: in 1998 there were 5.5 PAS deaths for every 10,000 total deaths, followed by 9.2 in 1999, 9.1 in 2000, 7.0 in 2001, 12.2 in 2002, 13.6 in 2003, 12.3, in 2004, and an estimated 12/10,000 in 2005.

The percentage of patients referred to a specialist for psychological evaluation beyond that done by a hospice team has declined, falling from 31% in 1998 to 5% in 2005.

Patient Characteristics

There were no statistically significant differences between Oregonians who used PAS in 2005 and those from prior years. . . .

Although year-to-year variations occur, certain demographic patterns have become evident over the past eight years. Males and females have been equally likely to take advantage of the DWDA. Divorced and never-married persons were more likely to use PAS than married and widowed residents. A higher level of education has been strongly associated with the use of PAS; Oregonians with a baccalaureate degree or higher were 7.9 times more likely to use PAS than those without a high school diploma. Conversely, several groups have emerged as being less likely to use PAS. These include people age 85 or older, people who did not graduate from high school, people who are married or widowed, and Oregon residents living east of the Cascade Range.

Patients with certain terminal illnesses were more likely to use PAS. The ratio of DWDA deaths to all deaths resulting from the same underlying illness was highest for three conditions: amyotrophic lateral sclerosis (ALS) (269.5 per 10,000), HIV/AIDS (218.3), and malignant neoplasms [cancer] (39.9). Among the causes associated with at least five deaths, the lowest rate (8.7) was for patients with chronic lower respiratory diseases (CLRD), such as emphysema.

During 2005, 36 patients died at home, and two died at assisted living facilities. All individuals had some form of health insurance. As in previous years, most (92%) of the patients who used PAS in 2005 were enrolled in hospice care. The median length of the patient-physician relationship was 8 weeks. . . .

End-of-Life Concerns

Providers were asked if, based on discussions with patients, any of seven end-of-life concerns might have contributed to the patients' requests for lethal medication. In nearly all cases, physicians reported multiple concerns contributing to the request. The most frequently reported concerns included a decreasing ability to participate in activities that make life enjoyable (89%), loss of dignity (89%), and losing autonomy (79%).

Since 2002, both the number of prescriptions written for physician-assisted suicide and the number of terminally ill patients taking lethal medication have remained relatively stable with about 1 in 800 deaths among Oregonians in 2005 resulting from physician-assisted suicide. A large population study of dying Oregonians published in 2004 found that 17% considered PAS seriously enough to have discussed the matter with their family and that about 2% of patients formally requested PAS. Of the 1,384 decedents for whom information was gathered, one had received a prescription for lethal medication and did not take it. No unreported cases of PAS were identified.

Overall, smaller numbers of patients appear to use PAS in Oregon compared to the Netherlands. However, . . . our numbers are based on a reporting system for terminally ill patients who legally receive prescriptions for lethal medications, and do not include patients and physicians who may act outside the provisions of the DWDA.

Over the last eight years, the rate of PAS among patients with ALS in Oregon has been substantially higher than among patients with other illnesses. This finding is consistent with other studies. In the Netherlands, where both PAS and euthanasia are openly practiced, one in five ALS patients died as a result of PAS or euthanasia. A study of Oregon and Washington ALS patients found that one-third of these patients discussed wanting PAS in the last month of life. Though numbers are small, and results must be interpreted with caution, Oregon HIV/AIDS patients are also more likely to use PAS.

Physicians have consistently reported that concerns about loss of autonomy, loss of dignity, and decreased ability to participate in activities that make life enjoyable as important motivating factors in patient requests for lethal medication across all eight years. Interviews with family members during 1999 corroborated physician reports. These findings were supported by a study of hospice nurses and social workers caring for PAS patients in Oregon.

While it may be common for patients with a terminal illness to consider PAS, a request for PAS can be an opportunity for a medical provider to explore with patients their fears and wishes around end-of-life care, and to make patients aware of other options. Often once the provider has addressed a patient's concerns, he or she may choose not to pursue PAS.

Physician-Assisted Suicide and Euthanasia Are Increasing in Europe

Colin Nickerson

Colin Nickerson is a reporter for the Boston Globe. *In the following selection he describes the increasing use of both assisted suicide and euthanasia in Europe. Voluntary euthanasia—mercy killing, by a doctor, of those who request it—is legal only in Holland and Belgium. Nickerson reports that opponents are afraid that terminally ill people may come to feel that it is selfish not to die. He also notes that opponents worry that euthanasia may spread to comatose patients and infants born with medical defects. In fact, seriously afflicted newborns are already sometimes euthanized in Holland. (Although this is in violation of existing law, the Dutch government is currently drawing up regulations under which it will be legal.) However, assisted suicide is much more common than euthanasia and is supported by a large majority of the population in some European countries. German and British patients who want to die often travel to Switzerland, Nickerson writes, where they can obtain help from Swiss organizations willing to prescribe lethal medication.*

Long famous for secretive banks and soaring peaks, Switzerland is now gaining a reputation as a death destination, a country where desperately ill people can come to kill themselves with help from organizations.

"What we do is no secret; we're proud of our work," said Ludwig Minelli, founder of Dignitas, a Zurich-based group that assists ailing Germans, Britons, and others who want to die. "Our purpose is to fight for the freedom of people to end their lives when their lives become unendurable" because of painful illness or old age, he said.

More than 2,000 people have received medically prescribed doses of barbiturates to kill themselves in Switzerland over the past 10 years, according to figures kept by the three main suicide organizations.

So-called assisted suicide is legal here as long as the agencies that arrange death do so for "honorable reasons," without seeking profit, although they may charge basic fees.

Dignitas has raised concerns among prosecutors in other European countries by facilitating the suicides of non-Swiss, a legal gray area, arranging everything from travel tickets to funeral services, as well as the fatal dose. Minelli said almost two-thirds of his clients come from Germany and Britain, where doctors are forbidden from helping patients end their lives.

Debate Is Widespread in Europe

The Swiss connection is just one part of a wider debate ringing across Europe, as doctors, ethicists, politicians, and "right to die" advocates square off over whether assisted suicide and even euthanasia—presently legal in just two countries, the Netherlands and Belgium—should be entitlements for the dying or the grievously ill. . . .

In Germany, the discussion carries the weight of the country's horrific mid-20th-century history. Under Hitler, doctor-administered death was official policy of a state obsessed with "genetic health." More than 250,000 infants, children, and adults with severe physical or mental disabilities were killed during the Nazi era, ostensibly to purify the Aryan race, according to historians.

Largely because of that history, medical professionals in Germany almost uniformly oppose "death by doctor," despite public opinion polls indicating that a huge majority of citizens—82 percent, according to one survey—favor legalization of assisted suicide.

A smaller percentage of the population supports Dutch-style medical euthanasia. Euthanasia is a mercy killing done directly by a doctor; assisted suicides are ones in which the deadly dose may be prescribed by the doctor or, as in Switzerland, obtained by a third party, but taken by the individual.

"We in Germany, with our history, should be most wary of promoting euthanasia or encouraging death," said Dr. Joerg-Dietrich Hoppe, president of the German Medical Association. "The killing of a person—and that, in the end, is what's at issue—should not be the duty of a doctor," he said. "The duty of a doctor is to preserve life and to restore health. When cure is impossible, the duty of the doctor is to alleviate suffering with palliative treatment, not a fatal dose."

Patients, Not Doctors, Should Choose

Advocates of assisted suicide and voluntary euthanasia insist that it is the ailing individual, not doctors, who should make the choice of whether to live or die.

"Any pluralistic society must allow every citizen to live this last act of their life, that of choosing their own death," said lawyer Jacqueline Herremans, head of Belgium's Association for the Right to Die with Dignity. "The feeling of the right to choose one's destiny is certainly growing in the [European] population."

The US Supreme Court decision has raised pressure on European lawmakers struggling to accommodate popular demands for a more permissive approach to ending life while preventing abuse.

Opponents of euthanasia and assisted suicide assert that the experiment in Holland has already gone awry and that doctors occasionally prescribe death for comatose patients, including those who have never stipulated a desire for death under a living will or some similar legal device, as well as for newborns with dreadful, but treatable, afflictions. . . .

Euthanasia Is Legal in Holland and Belgium

In 2001, the Netherlands legalized not only assisted suicide but also euthanasia. Doctors are authorized to directly administer lethal injections or pills to cogent, terminally ill people or to individuals in "lasting, unendurable pain" who prefer fast death to an agonizing battle. About 3,800 Dutch a year opt for a fatal injection from a physician or a prescribed toxic overdose.

Belgium also permits voluntary euthanasia for people of sound mind but "futile medical condition." In both countries, medical groups insist rigorous guidelines are followed.

Opponents say that huge danger lies in the moral and social pressures they believe are created by legalized euthanasia and, to a lesser extent, assisted suicide. In Holland especially, critics maintain, euthanasia has become such an accepted medical procedure that people who don't choose to die this way may be seen as selfishly using medical resources that could better help curable patients.

"Poor Grandfather, dying of cancer, may come to feel he should quicken the process, almost as his civic duty," said Hoppe. "Even loving families can be manipulated into thinking that quick death is always preferable to lingering death. But perhaps Grandpa wants a few more weeks or months, even in pain."

Newborns Have Been Euthanized in Holland

Critics further say that once euthanasia becomes accepted practice for consenting adults, it inevitably raises thorny questions of whether to permit mercy killings of comatose patients or even newborns with terrible deformities. . . . Dutch doctors have euthanized small numbers of infants born with severe afflictions, in technical violation of both the country's euthanasia law and the pledges made by politicians and activists who pushed for it. . . . The practice continues under a set of protocols that, in essence, remove the risk of prosecution for doctors who follow medical guidance and report the procedure. The newborn must be perceived to be suffering greatly with no hope of improvement, and the parents must give permission. Mercy killings are administered to between 15 and 20 infants a year in Holland, according to medical studies. . . .

Euthanasia for other "people of no free will," including comatose patients and severely retarded or demented individuals suffering great pain from a terminal illness, remains a legal gray area in Holland. But medical studies quoted by European news media indicate that roughly 1,000 such individuals are euthanized in the Netherlands every year.

Assisted Suicides Are Spreading

In Britain, a bill introduced [in 2006] in the House of Lords would grant a "competent" individual suffering from incurable illness or unbearable pain the legal right to demand that doctors prescribe a lethal cocktail, although the patient would be required to administer the dose himself.

Archbishop Peter Smith of the Roman Catholic Archdiocese of Cardiff recently called the bill "assisted killing" and said he believes the government could better help the dying by providing more money for hospices and institutions offering palliative care.

In Switzerland, suicide is legal, and the national penal code exempts from legal penalty those who help people kill themselves, so long as the assistance is rendered for "honorable" reasons, such as bringing an end to suffering. This loophole has allowed groups like Dignitas to function as charities whose mission is to streamline the suicide process.

"We offer a solution for people in a dilemma, people either in great pain or fearful of slipping into dementia and becoming incapable of making their own final decisions," Minelli said.

Dignitas has helped 493 individuals kill themselves since 1998, more than half of them coming from Germany and Britain. Investigators in those countries have alleged that Dignitas has arranged the deaths of people who were neither dying nor even terribly ill.

"We do not want this travel agency of death," Elisabeth Heister-Neumann, justice minister for the German state of Lower Saxony, where Dignitas recently opened an office, told the *Die Welt* newspaper. "The fear of pain requires treatment for pain, not death."

Meanwhile, a prominent teaching hospital in Switzerland [in January 2006] became the first to allow assisted suicides on its premises under highly limited circumstances. The Vaud University Hospital Center in Lausanne will now permit terminally ill patients who have expressed a "consistent desire" to die before entering the hospital, but who are too incapacitated to go home to take their own lives with help from Exit, another assisted-suicide group.

"It was a difficult decision. The mission of our hospital is to cure patients, not help them die," said Alberto Crespo, legal and ethical director of the hospital. "But we have to respect the wishes of those patients who want to die, yet are unable to leave the hospital. We cannot deprive them of a right they would have at home, simply because they are in a hospital."

CHAPTER 2

Withdrawal of Life-Sustaining Medical Treatment

Medical Treatment Should Be Withdrawn Only When Burdensome to the Patient

President's Council on Bioethics

The President's Council on Bioethics was created by President George W. Bush to advise him on ethical issues related to advances in biomedical science and technology. In the following selection the council declares its strong opposition to assisted suicide and euthanasia. However, it also states that the goal of ethical caregiving is to benefit the patient's life, not to postpone death as long as is medically possible. Therefore, medical intervention that is useless or burdensome to the patient should be avoided. The council specifically affirms that feeding tubes are not always obligatory and that palliative care involving a risk of earlier death is acceptable.

Euthanasia and assisted suicide are antithetical to ethical caregiving for people with disability. These practices should always be opposed.

If we are to care well for the needs and interests of persons incapable of caring for themselves, we must erect and defend certain moral boundaries that prevent us from violating the people entrusted to our care: No euthanasia, no assisted suicide. These practices should be opposed for many reasons, and not only because of our moral (and legal) opposition to seeking the death and taking the life of innocent human beings. These taboos are also indispensable for giving good care: one cannot think wholeheartedly about how best to care for the life the patient now has if ending his or her life becomes, for us, always an eligible treatment option. This holds true not only in . . . vexing end-of-life cases. . . . It is also indispensable

President's Council on Bioethics, "Taking Care: Ethical Caregiving in Our Aging Society," www.bioethics.gov, September, 2005.

for fulfilling our everyday obligations and performing our everyday ministrations in their care. It is indispensable to serving faithfully and loyally, deserving of the trust that has been reposed in us, whether as family members or as doctors, nurses, and hospice workers. A decent society will not seriously consider abandoning and betraying its most vulnerable and disabled members. A prudent society will not weaken those necessary restraints that prevent even the most devoted caregivers from yielding—out of weakness or frustration—to the temptation to abandon or betray those in need of their care.

Try as we may to be devoted caregivers, we are not saints, and—under the pressure of trying circumstances—even our best motives may lead us to betray or abandon altogether those who in their vulnerability depend on our care. Hence, we all need a shared moral world in which certain actions that undermine the solidarity of the human community are firmly beyond the pale. Or, to put the matter positively, it is only as we deny ourselves the option of "solving" intransigent social problems by ridding ourselves of those who manifest the problem, that we can train ourselves to cultivate with greater clarity and wisdom the capacities we have and the virtues we need for caregiving. A society that sets its face against abandoning those whose lives are in decline has a better chance of being a society that thinks creatively about the trajectory of life and the bonds between the generations, of remaining a society in which to live long is also to live well together.

The Goal Is to Benefit the Patient, Not Postpone Death

The goal of ethical caregiving in the clinical setting is not to extend the length or postpone the end of the patient's life as long as is medically possible, but always to benefit the life the patient still has.

In caring for those who cannot care for themselves, our primary goal is to do everything we reasonably can to *benefit* their lives—from meeting basic needs and sustaining life, to easing pain and curing ailments, to offering comfort in difficult times and, in the end, keeping company in the face of looming death. Medical interventions that sustain life are, of course, often a benefit to those whose lives they sustain. But extending life and delaying death are not the only or primary goals that should guide caregivers, and there are times in which pursuing those goals would require imposing new and unjustified burdens on the patient. Caring well for the patient does not require *always* choosing interventions that would prolong his life or delay his dying, and sometimes best care requires forgoing treatments that may sustain life at the cost of imposing undue misery or offering palliative care that accepts an increased risk of an earlier death. Some interventions, even if life-sustaining, do not benefit the life the patient now has. Some interventions, aimed at benefiting the patient's present life, may not be life-extending.

Moreover, in caring for the life the patient now has, we care also for the manner and humanity of his dying. Feeding tubes and respirators are not always obligatory. Neither is hospitalization or the intensive care unit. And if these measures are used for a time, there are circumstances when it is morally permissible—and even, perhaps, morally required—to desist. Dying as well as possible—or, more modestly, in as little misery as possible—is also one of our concerns and cares. Even as we must never seek or aim at the patient's death, so we are also under a positive obligation not to impose treatments that would unduly burden the patient, make his dying more difficult, or otherwise deprive him of a more peaceful end of life or of final hours in the company of those who love him. Dying, like living, is a human matter, not merely a medical or technological one.

Any Treatment Burdensome to the Patient Should Be Withheld

The clearest ethical grounds for forgoing life sustaining treatments are an obligation to avoid inflicting treatments that are *unduly burdensome to the patient being treated* and an obligation to avoid treatments that are not at all (or not any longer) efficacious in attaining their desired result.

As caregivers, with necessarily limited powers to fix what is broken, we must distinguish between the burdens of disease (which we cannot always control) and the burdens of treatment (for which we are fully responsible). There are some burdens and some forms of suffering that we cannot make disappear, despite our best efforts. Because our powers of cure are limited, sometimes all we can do is stand with the patient in her days of trial, always seeking to minimize those burdens we cannot fully eradicate. But *where we do intervene* with medical treatments or dislocations required to obtain them, we are under an obligation not to add unduly to the patient's existing miseries and troubles. And, of course, we are also under an obligation not to intervene uselessly. Those interventions that cause undue burden or fail to benefit the life the patient still has can be, and often clearly should be, forgone. Judging when this is the case is always the task of prudent caregivers, making conscientious decisions in particular circumstances for particular patients.

Withdrawal of Feeding Tubes Is Euthanasia

Anthony Ozimic and John Fleming

Anthony Ozimic is the political secretary of the Society for the Protection of Unborn Children, a British anti-abortion organization. John Fleming is a Catholic priest, president of Campion College in Australia, and an adjunct professor at the Southern Cross Bioethics Institute. The following selection is an argument they wrote in opposition to the bill that legalized advance directives—so-called "living wills"—in Britain. Prior to the passage of this bill in 2005, British people, unlike U.S. citizens, could not draw up legal documents stating what medical care they would want, or who they would want to make medical decisions if they became incapacitated. In the opinion of Ozimic and Fleming, withholding or withdrawing nutrition and hydration (feeding tubes), even if requested in an advance directive, is "euthanasia by neglect" and should not be allowed. This used to be called "passive euthanasia," although that term is now rarely used because it implies killing rather than allowing death to come naturally. Ozmic and Fleming feel that withdrawal of life support is killing. Furthermore, they do not believe that assisted nutrition and hydration should be considered "medical treatment," even though courts in both Britain and the United States have ruled that it is treatment.

Many people concerned about human rights, medical ethics and the rights of the elderly and disabled have over many years continually voiced their opposition to the withholding or withdrawal of nutrition and hydration from a patient so as to cause the patient's death. Such intentional killings are rightly termed "euthanasia" or "euthanasia by

Anthony Ozimic and John Fleming, "What Is Euthanasia by Neglect and Why Is It Wrong?" Society for the Protection of Unborn Children, www.spuc.org.uk. Reproduced by permission.

omission". . . . In an open letter published in the [London] *Daily Telegraph* in July 2001, 11 respected medics and medicolegal lawyers said: ". . .the withdrawing and withholding of treatment from patients, particularly hydration and nutrition, is a matter of prime public concern."

There are few moral convictions more deeply ingrained than the sanctity of human life, and there is no stronger human instinct than self-preservation. The purpose of the law is to protect fundamental human values, fundamental human rights. One of the ways in which the law fulfils this purpose is by insisting that those who exercise power over life and death of their fellow human beings must not intentionally cause the death of an innocent human being. However, any law passed to legalise euthanasia by neglect sends a signal to society that the lives of the mentally incapacitated are not worth living, indeed that the law implicitly recommends that they should be killed. Is it right for the law to tell the most vulnerable members of our society that they would be better off dead? Should the "survival of the fittest" really be the character, the ethos, the ethics of our society?

Until now we have always said "no", and our legal prohibition on killing the innocent extends to intentionally killing by omission. That is, unlawful killing under English law includes both acts and omissions. In the 1993 Bland case, Lord Justice Hoffman noted that: "If someone allows a small child or invalid in his care to starve to death, we do not say that he allowed nature to take its course. We think that he has committed a particularly wicked crime. We treat him as if he had introduced an external agency of death. It is the same ethical principle which requires doctors and hospitals to provide patients in their care with such medical attention and nursing as they are reasonably able to give. The giving of food to a needy person is so much the quintessential example of kindness and humanity that it is hard to imagine a case in which it would be morally right to withhold it."

Many patients who can receive sustenance orally are given it through nasogastric or gastrostomy tubes for convenience. However, the judges in the Bland case redefined tube-feeding as "medical treatment" and allowed medical staff to withdraw it from PVS [persistent vegetative state] patient Tony Bland, who then died of dehydration. The Bland judgement was a total reversal of traditional medical ethics, a disturbing departure from the common law and legislation by judicial fiat. Lord Mustill noted that the judgement left the law "morally and intellectually misshapen".

Nutrition and hydration (assisted or otherwise) are always of benefit to the patient, regardless of the person's 'quality of life'. The only exceptions to this are where nutrition and hydration and/or their physical administration are physically burdensome or impossible, when the patient can no longer assimilate them, or where the benefit may be negligible, e.g. where death is imminent. The withholding or withdrawal of nutrition and hydration from a non-dying patient who is able to assimilate them can only result in the premature death of the patient by starvation and dehydration, a death at once unpleasant and drawn out. (This may also apply to a terminally-ill patient, depending upon the prognosis.) Such euthanasia by omission is contrary to the fundamental principle of medical ethics: primum non nocere—first, do no harm.

Four Principles of Medical Ethics

One popular account of medical ethics, makes an appeal to "the four principles":

1. non-maleficence (to avoid harm)
2. beneficence (to do good)
3. autonomy (the right to act freely) and
4. justice (acting fairly towards the patient).

Leaving aside the obvious shortcomings of such an abbreviated approach to medical ethics, we can nevertheless see how euthanasia by neglect violates all four principles:

1. Euthanasia by neglect is maleficent: it causes harm by killing a patient through a very long drawn out process of starvation and dehydration, a process which is uncomfortable and painful for the patient.

2. Euthanasia by neglect cannot be beneficent: A doctor is ethically and legally obliged to act in a patient's best interests. Intentionally killing the patient by neglect of reasonable care can never be in the patient's best interests.

3. Euthanasia by neglect extinguishes the autonomy of patients and diminishes the autonomy of doctors. Autonomy is not an absolute the exercise of which trumps all other considerations. The patient must exercise his or her right to autonomy in a responsible and ethically sound manner. Both ethics and the law say that, just as we cannot sell ourselves into slavery, we cannot consent to be murdered. This is because the right to life, like the right to liberty, is inalienable. The obligation to respect the right to life extends to respecting one's own life. It is unethical to intentionally deprive oneself of life. Making euthanasia by neglect available to patients would lead to pressure on doctors and nurses to assist suicide and intentionally kill their patients by neglect. The effect of this is to significantly diminish their autonomy to practise their professional arts ethically, and according to their consciences and the Hippocratic Oath. Legalising assisted suicide and intentional killing by neglect of reasonable care turns a class of private citizens into public killers. It changes doctors and nurses from being healers and carers into poisoners and killers.

4. Euthanasia by neglect violates justice, the requirement to treat all patients impartially and to be fair when allocating health care resources. The possibility of euthanasia by neglect would lead to pressure (real or perceived) on the elderly and the chronically ill to cease being a burden on society, on the health service, and on their relatives. Legalising euthanasia by neglect reduces the patient from being an individual to whom the doctor has a professional obligation, into a utile, a unit in a utilitarian system of healthcare rationing, with an implied duty to die if they became too difficult or time-consuming or expensive to treat.

Autonomy or an Excuse to Kill?

Doctors are required to consider each individual patient's best interests. However, it is often wrongly assumed that the only way to determine best interests is to find out what they wanted before they became incapacitated. 'Best interests' are not always based on the choices a patient makes, or might have made before they became incapacitated. Failing to observe the incompetent person's wishes does not necessarily imply disrespect for the individual or contravene his or her rights. Doctors often need to make treatment decisions against the patient's wishes, but in their best interests, e.g. when a patient asks for a prescription, the doctor will consider whether or not it will benefit the patient. Autonomy, while being important, is not the only interest a patient has. Their other interests include life and health, and the provision of a reasonable standard of health care to support life and health. These interests become especially important if a person becomes incapacitated, a circumstance in which the patient can no longer exercise autonomy. Regardless of any decrease in autonomy, an incapacitated person still has intrinsic dignity and a right to live simply by virtue of being human.

Another danger is that an emphasis on advance decisions shifts the focus towards a concept of quality of life. It is true that considerations of quality of life can help make decisions which are in the patient's best interests, e.g. doctors are not required to provide treatments which are burdensome, disproportionate to benefit, even if they serve to keep a patient alive. However, the crucial fact is that being killed is never in a patient's best interests. Any system using advance decisions must prevent them being used to bring about the deaths of patients. . . .

A third danger is if the exercise of autonomy is handed over to a person exercising a lasting power of attorney. Such a proxy decision-maker would not need to be medically or legally qualified; would not be legally accountable for the consequences of whatever advice or instructions that he may give to medical staff; and may benefit in some way, especially financially, from the patient's death. Such a proxy decision-maker might order the patient to be deprived of care or treatment on the grounds that the incapacitated patient "wouldn't want to live like this". So the concept of autonomy would become corrupted to a concept of substituted judgment and euthanasia would become an option even if the patient had not asked for it. Only the senior clinician in charge is fully qualified to make decisive judgements as to the appropriate medical care and treatment for the patient. This does not mean that the patient may be subjected to whatever treatments and decisions the doctors care to make. The doctor must seek only and always the patient's restoration of health, preservation of life, prevention of impairment and alleviation from suffering.

Euthanasia by neglect is unethical and its legalisation would degrade the moral character of patients and doctors and pervert the purpose of medicine, which is health. It is a macabre type of medicine that kills instead of cures.

Withdrawal of Feeding Tubes Is Not Euthanasia

Paul Lauritzen

Paul Lauritzen is a professor in the Religious Studies department and director of the Program in Applied Ethics at John Carroll University in Cleveland, Ohio. In the following selection, he argues that withdrawal of feeding tubes is not euthanasia because euthanasia implies an intent to kill, whereas failure to feed a patient artificially is simply to be aware that in nature the ability to eat and drink normally leads to death. To let nature take its course in such a case is to acknowledge that death is a natural fact of life, not a choice made by humans.

The old adage that hard cases make bad law is often true, but it is also true that hard cases can help crystallize fundamental moral issues. Thus, at the risk of reviving the painful passions that swirled around Terri Schiavo's death, I want to ask whether that incredibly hard case helps us identify core moral questions about end-of-life decisions.

Can we learn anything morally useful from the Schiavo case [in which her husband fought to have her feeding tubes removed]? For example, was the strong, public opposition among some prominent Catholics, including some bishops, to the removal of Schiavo's feeding and hydration tubes an indication that church teaching about end-of-life care has changed?

To answer these questions, we need to look carefully at the claims of those who condemned the removal of Schiavo's feeding tube as morally repugnant, for behind the highly charged rhetoric that frequently accompanied such condem-

Paul Lauritzen, "Caring at the End," *Commonweal*, vol. CXXXIII, March 10, 2006. Copyright © 2006 Commonweal Foundation. Reproduced by permission of Commonweal Foundation.

nations rests a core moral conviction that bears examination. Consider, for example, the claims made by various hierarchical officials and their spokespersons, both here and abroad. Bishop Robert Vasa of Baker, Oregon, said that it would be "murder" to remove Schiavo's feeding tube. Cathy Cleaver Ruse, the director of planning and information for the Prolife Office of the United States Conference of Catholic Bishops (USCCB), suggested that Schiavo was executed, and Cardinal Javier Lozano Barragan, the head of the Pontifical Council for Health Care, claimed that Schiavo was not allowed to die, but was killed. To put these claims in terms of traditional Catholic moral teaching, all three are, in effect, saying that removing the feeding tube from Schiavo was an act of euthanasia, which the church explicitly condemns.

Was Terri Schiavo Euthanized?

To see what assumptions are embedded in the claim that Schiavo was euthanized, it is useful to consider the definition of euthanasia set out in the Vatican's 1980 Declaration on Euthanasia. According to the declaration, euthanasia is "an action or an omission which of itself or by intention causes death, in order that all suffering may in this way be eliminated. Euthanasia's terms of reference, therefore, are to be found in the intention of the will and in the methods used."

Framed in this way, the Schiavo case throws into sharp relief a central moral question raised by the prospect of withdrawing a feeding tube from any patient in a persistent vegetative state (PVS). Do we inevitably intend death when we remove a feeding tube from a PVS patient? Many critics of the action Michael Schiavo (Terri's husband) took have wanted to answer yes. Take, for example, bioethicist Gilbert Meilaender's exchange with Robert D. Orr in the August/September 2004 issue of *First Things*. According to Meilaender, Christians have traditionally said that treatment may be removed from patients when the treatment is either useless or excessively burdensome. The problem in the case of PVS patients is that, almost by definition, a feeding tube cannot be burdensome to the patient, and it does not appear to be useless. As Meilaender puts it, given that a feeding tube "may preserve for years the life of this living human being," how can the treatment be said to be useless? Given that a person in a persistent vegetative state is, strictly speaking, not dying, it is hard to see how we could be merely letting that person die when we remove the feeding tube. Indeed, says Meilaender, in the circumstance of removing a feeding tube from a PVS patient, we seem not to be aiming to end a useless treatment, but to end a useless life. And this is precisely what Christians must resist.

I will come back to this point shortly, but it is important to see that Meilaender is not alone in making this argument. I suspect, for example, that something like this conviction stands behind the claims of the many Catholic commentators who cited Pope John Paul II's March 2004 allocution on nutrition and hydration in opposing the removal of Schiavo's feeding tube. And, indeed, it is worth looking at the papal statement with this in mind. . . .

In the key passage, John Paul makes two claims. First, providing nutrition and hydration is a form of care, not a form of treatment. Second, withdrawing a feeding tube is essentially to aim at death. With regard to the second point, he said: "Death by starvation or dehydration is, in fact, the only possible outcome as a result of this withdrawal. In this sense it ends up becoming, if done knowingly and willingly, true and proper euthanasia by omission."

What should we make of this claim? The first thing to note is what is not being said. John Paul does not assert that removing a feeding tube is directly to kill the patient. In terms of the definition of euthanasia set out in the Declaration on Euthanasia, removing a feeding tube is not an action "which of itself" causes death. This is important because if removing the feeding tube is not wrong per se, then, if it is wrong, it must be so because of the intention of the will in removing the tube. (Recall that the declaration defines euthanasia in reference to "the intention of the will and in the methods used.")

Death Is a Natural Fact of Life

This distinction takes us back to Meilaender's claim that in removing a feeding tube from a PVS patient we necessarily aim at death. Is Meilaender right about this? It certainly appears to be a plausible claim. After all, as both Meilaender and John Paul note, death is the certain outcome of removing the feeding tube from a PVS patient, a patient who is not imminently dying. Yet appearances can be deceiving.

No one has diagnosed the confusion here more perceptively than [bioethicist] Daniel Callahan in his important book, *The Troubled Dream of Life.* According to Callahan, modern medicine has come to see death as an enemy that must be fought by any and all means. And because medicine has been so enormously successful in combating the causes of early death and thereby lengthening the average life span, we have come increasingly to act as if death is not a natural fact of life, but a failure of human will. From a traditional fatalism in the face of the biological realities of human embodiment, we have moved to a moralism that condemns every concession to human finitude as a moral failing. Indeed, says Callahan, we have lost any sense of nature as acting independently of human choice, as if no death that could have been prevented could be anything other than the result of an intentional act.

Thus, to say that removing a feeding tube from a PVS patient is necessarily to aim at death is to conflate human action and natural events. It is to fail to recognize that dying is commonly associated biologically with a natural inability to eat or drink. If we do not conflate human and natural causality, it is perfectly sensible to say that a person suffering from a severe brain injury who cannot eat or drink is in fact dying, even if

we can intervene and postpone that dying for years. Not starting or stopping artificial nutrition and hydration in such a
case is not necessarily to aim at death, though one could intend death in such circumstances.

Should Technology Determine
What We Ought to Do?

To conclude otherwise, it seems to me, is to succumb to a sort
of hubris that repudiates any natural limits on human action.
Callahan has captured the irony of this situation perfectly. "In
the name of the sanctity of life, many who would consider
themselves conservative and supporters of traditional religious
values are forced into a slavery to medical possibilities, held in
thrall by the false gods of technology." The irony is particularly striking in relation to the Catholic commentators
(Meilaender is not Catholic) who appear to adopt the
Promethean attitude toward human embodiment and finitude
that the tradition has long rejected.

There was a time when it would have been possible for
Catholic writers, with the full weight of magisterial teaching
behind them, to say that a life lived in a state of permanent
unconsciousness with no apparent hope for a spiritual or social life was a terrible prospect, one that no person was obligated to embrace. In traditional Catholic teaching about the
end of life, letting nature take its course in such a case made
sense, not because such a life was regarded as worthless, but
because in such a circumstance we confront the limits of human powers in the face of human vulnerability.

Both the view that providing nutrition and hydration for
PVS patients is morally obligatory, and the position that providing a feeding tube is a form of care and not treatment, represent a shift in Catholic teaching. Understandably, commentators who have noted this shift have sought to downplay its
significance, perhaps hoping that the change will be confined
to cases involving persistent vegetative states. My own view,

though, is that the changes are much more profound than anyone has acknowledged. . . . When natural constraints on human actions are treated so cavalierly, when what we can technically do appears to determine what we ought to do, the wisdom of the tradition that recognizes the goodness of our embodied existence and the fact that mere existence is not an ultimate good, seems to have been lost. If the ordeal of the Terri Schiavo case helps us to recognize the possibility of such a loss, it will not have been in vain.

Religious Views About Withdrawal of Feeding Tubes Do Not Agree

Teresa Watanabe and Larry B. Stammer

Teresa Watanabe and Larry B. Stammer are staff writers for the Los Angeles Times. In the following selection they present views of many religions toward the removal of feeding tubes from dying or vegetative patients. The authors note that differing opinions are held, even among people of the same faith, depending on whether they view feeding tubes as nourishment or as medical treatment. Thus, individual Jewish and Christian opinions vary. The Islamic view is that withdrawing a feeding tube is euthanasia, whereas Buddhists support ending artificial feeding if recovery is hopeless. Hindus believe that it depends on individual circumstances.

The Terri Schiavo case [in which her husband fought to have her feeding tubes removed] has sharply divided bioethicists from secular and religious traditions over what they say is the key ethical dilemma: Should artificial nutrition be considered food or medicine? Those who view it as food argue that withholding it from Schiavo would be as immoral as leaving a helpless infant to starve. But those who regard it as medicine say that, given the Florida woman's condition, it is as ethical to withdraw the feeding tube as it would be to shut down a respirator.

The question, fraught with emotions over the nature of human life and obligations to safeguard it, has riven people within the same religion.

Rabbi Elliot Dorff, rector of the University of Judaism in Los Angeles, argued that artificial nutrition was not food but

Teresa Watanabe and Larry B. Stammer, "Diverse Faiths Find No Easy Answers," *Los Angeles Times*, March 25, 2005. Reproduced by permission.

medical treatment and was appropriate to withdraw given the hopelessness of Schiavo's persistent vegetative state. He also said people had to accept their mortality, as the Bible made clear.

But Rabbi Avram Reisner, a member along with Dorff of a Jewish law committee in the Conservative Movement, said the feeding tube was removed prematurely. If Schiavo could be trained to swallow, a capacity he said had not been adequately explored, then feeding her with a spoon would be morally obligated. Until that issue was resolved, he said, artificial nutrition should have been maintained. "Feeding is part of the natural process of life," Reisner said.

Orthodox Jews voiced even stronger views. Withholding food and drink was "cruel and unusual punishment," said Rabbi Yitzchok Adlerstein, chairman of Jewish law and ethics at Loyola Law School in Los Angeles.

Christians Disagree

Similar divisions are evident among Roman Catholics. The Vatican and U.S. bishops have said that giving food and drink, even artificially, was morally required in the case of Schiavo, who is Catholic.

But ethics professor Daniel C. Maguire at Marquette University, a Catholic school in Milwaukee, took issue with that position. Saying the Vatican and U.S. bishops were out of step with mainstream Catholic theology against extraordinary measures to sustain life, Maguire called the Schiavo case a "15-year atrocity" that represented a tendency to idealize physical life and forget the natural process of death. "We live in a culture where death is the witch or warlock to be driven out of town—by technical means if possible," Maguire said.

Conflicting opinions also exist among evangelical Christians, many of whom have sided with court appeals by Schiavo's parents to continue feeding the severely brain-damaged woman.

Focus on the Family, a conservative evangelical broadcast ministry in Colorado Springs, Colo., said it was "appalled and opposed" to removing Schiavo's feeding tube. "This is a woman who was not dying until they removed that feeding tube," said Carrie Gordon Earll, the ministry's senior analyst for bioethics. She maintained that Schiavo was not brain dead or in a persistent vegetative state.

But evangelical Scott Rae, a professor of Christian ethics at Biola University in La Mirada, argued that withdrawing the feeding tube would be appropriate if it could be determined that it coincided with Schiavo's wishes. He said he agreed with a 1990 U.S. Supreme Court decision that feeding tubes "constituted medical treatment analogous to ventilation, and removing them was no more starving someone than removing ventilation was suffocating someone." He said he would not want to be sustained as Schiavo had been. "As a Christian, I don't want anybody to delay my homecoming" in heaven, he said.

But Rae said he was not convinced that Schiavo would have willed this outcome, and questioned whether her husband, Michael Schiavo, was acting in her best interests. So long as her parents were willing and able to care for her, what was the harm in allowing them to do so, he asked. "If in doubt, you always offer life," Rae said.

The Schiavo case has triggered discussion and soul searching in other religious communities as well.

Islamic, Buddhist, and Hindu Views

Southern California physician Hassan Hathout said Islamic ethics asserted a right to food and drink and that withdrawing Schiavo's feeding tube was "tantamount to euthanasia by hunger and thirst, which is a very cruel kind of euthanasia."

Tibetan Buddhists believe that prolonging someone in a vegetative state could harm the chances of a good rebirth, and they would support ending artificial feeding if recovery were hopeless, said Robert Thurman, a Columbia University professor of Indo-Tibetan Buddhist studies.

"Natural death is very natural and healthy, which means no lifeline like that," said Bishop Koshin Ogui of the San Francisco-based Buddhist Churches of America.

Other traditions, such as Hindu and Bahai, do not offer clear guidance for such modern ethical dilemmas, their practitioners said.

Lina Gupta, professor and philosophy department chair at Glendale Community College, said the Hindu response would depend on individual circumstances. Although not specifically addressing the Schiavo case, she said her tradition offered absolute moral dictates and flexible ones—for instance, eschewing killing in general but recognizing warriors who do so to protect others.

Saradeshaprana, a nun of the Vedanta Society in Los Angeles, said that the Hindu response would depend largely on the motivation for taking out the feeding tube and whether it would prolong or terminate Schiavo's suffering. Without knowing that, there was no clear answer, she said.

The California Legislature and the courts have defined artificial feeding tubes as medical treatment that can be withdrawn by wishes of the patient or a designated decision maker, said Vicki Michel, a Loyola Law School adjunct professor who coordinated a consortium of hospital ethics committees in Southern California. "On a gut emotional level, feeding someone is considered to be basic care," she said. "But people have to realize that when you put in a tube to artificially feed, it is a medical treatment unlike giving a spoon or baby bottle."

The Case of Terri Schiavo Raises Questions About Public Policy

Bruce Jennings

Bruce Jennings is a senior research scholar at the Hastings Center, an independent, nonpartisan, nonprofit bioethics research institute. This selection is part of a presentation he delivered there on the bitter controversy over Terri Schiavo, a woman who lingered in a vegetative state until a court ordered that her feeding tube be removed as directed by her husband. Schiavo died soon after in 2005. Jennings provides a summary of her case, then explains that there were several levels to the controversy, not only those concerning ethics and legal issues, but the unprecedented role of the media in the debate. In his opinion, the public needs to gain a better understanding of vegetative states and neurological functions so as to interpret what is discussed in the media. A still more important aspect of the Schiavo controversy, Jennings states, is what it revealed about American society and about the failure of both citizens and political leaders to handle the debate in a mature fashion.

[Terri Schiavo] fell unconscious in 1990, and over the course of many years, starting in 1993, her husband wanted to forgo artificial nutrition and hydration and life support for her on the grounds that she would not want to be kept alive this way. Her mother and father, the Schindler family, disagreed with Mr. Schiavo, and a controversy began in 1993 that lasted over a decade, going back and forth in the courts many times.

The courts were willing to affirm Mr. Schiavo's authority to make those decisions. Questions were raised about her true

Bruce Jennings, "The Long Dying Terri Schiavo—Private Tragedy, Public Danger," Presentation at The Hastings Center.org, May 20, 2005. Reproduced by permission.

prognosis, and the courts wanted to take a very careful look at that. Questions were raised about what she really wanted, what her wishes were. The courts wanted to take a very careful look at that. And so it went back for rehearing numerous times, but each time, the result was pretty much the same—the courts reaffirmed Mr. Schiavo's position rather than the Schindlers' position. The tube was removed twice, and reinserted twice.

The second time it was reinserted because—and now things started to superheat politically and this is what made the Schiavo case different from its predecessors—Governor [Jeb] Bush of Florida and the Florida state legislature passed a special law just to insert Terri's feeding tube. Some time later the Florida Supreme Court declared that statute ("Terri's Law") to be unconstitutional.

Just as the Florida state government got into the act in a big way, so did the federal government as the U.S. Congress passed and President George Bush signed a hastily considered federal law targeting the Schiavo case. This law was not as blatantly directive as the Florida law had been. It did not say: "Put the tube back in." Instead it paved the way for the Schindler family to take their lawsuit to the federal courts, perhaps in the hope that the federal courts would not be limited by the legal framework we have been discussing. But, to the surprise of some, the federal courts took a look at it, and said, "The State courts are right. We're not going to reverse them." And so finally, at the end of the day, the state court in Florida yet again ordered the feeding tube be removed in accordance with Mr. Schiavo's instructions. And it was, and Terri Schiavo died several days later.

Several Levels to the Controversy

There are several levels to this controversy. I've already mentioned the first level. There were bitter disputes about the nature of her illness, the nature of the diagnosis and prognosis, what her wishes were, whether her prior wishes were reliable—perhaps her current wishes would be different—and then there was a very bitter attack on Mr. Schiavo and his fitness to be a surrogate decisionmaker.

These questions tended to be more questions of fact. At a somewhat more conceptually complex level, there were powerful controversies going on in this case that reverberate throughout our society still about the relative value of the meaningfulness and quality of life to the person who's living it, versus the sanctity of life, regardless of how impaired or how limited that life might be. . . .

Whose life is it anyway? How about the state's? The state has the inherent power to protect life and health; is that where we should turn in end-of-life cases, especially when a very intense minority wants to see life prolonged? It is ironic that people who consider themselves conservative in this case were the ones who wanted to give this power to the government. Standing behind this seeming inconsistency is the fact that many religious persons and groups in our society believe that this decision to forgo life-sustaining treatment is an inappropriate decision for us to be making because it is encroaching on something that is not ours to decide. From some religious perspectives, if not all, we do not belong to ourselves. I don't understand why this same type of perspective would not just as readily instruct us not to use these machines, for that too is putting human will in the place of divine will. But in any case the machines were in place and so taking them out was the practical question, and many people resist that. (Because long-term prognosis cannot be determined immediately after a person's injury, artificial feeding tubes must be inserted to sustain the unconscious person who may not progress into PVS [persistent vegetative state] but who may instead recover consciousness.)

Artificial nutrition and hydration is something we can talk about: do we agree with the legal framework that says it is just another kind of treatment, or is it something special?

Then we have all kinds of interesting questions that have never been seen before in these kinds of cases. The fierceness of the controversy over what was wrong with Terri Schiavo was striking. But more striking to me still was the way that the video tapes and web sites played a role in this controversy in a way they never had before. One curious thing about the permanent vegetative state is that it involves destruction of the higher structures of the brain, but not the brain stem. It is not the same as brain death. People in PVS can breathe. Heart beat, lung function, and other biological functions continue. Also people in PVS are not asleep or unconscious. They're apparently awake. They go through wake and sleep cycles, and much of the time their eyes are open. And if you watch them, they have movements that are seemingly responses to stimuli in the environment around them.

Medicine is not so advanced a science that experts never disagree. But the overwhelming weight of opinion among neurologists is that these are reflexes only and don't signify awareness. Others who observe or care for these patients—family members, for example, sometimes nurses—often come to believe that there may be some awareness in there, that there is something behind the eyes. What is observation and what is projection, seeing what one desperately wants to see? ... I think we must trust and rely on our diagnostic technology and the experience of those most expert, not because they are infallible but because there is no reasonable alternative. Otherwise we will keep individuals in PVS on life-support machines until their bodies begin to decompose.

Impact of the Media

Nonetheless, these are difficult issues of knowledge, prudence; issues challenging in the calmest of times, but exceedingly difficult when weighed down with intense emotions. . . . Facts may batter beliefs with refutations without weakening them. During the Schiavo case we tried to ask ourselves in public:

What counts as evidence? What counts as science and reason? It was not handled at all well. Not in the shouting matches of the media talk shows. Not online, which is more of an information dirt road than an information superhighway. In this instance, public debate did little to enhance public understanding.

What made the Schiavo case different was the use and power of the image. Her image. Video tapes aired on the media and endlessly looping on websites. Hours of footage edited to show a few moments of behavior, reaction, or reflex. One of the things we need to do in the future is to work on our understanding as a society of some of these neurological conditions and to become much more sophisticated consumers of their visual representation. Should we also talk about privacy? It ceases to exist in this context.

Also, many other end of life cases are somewhat ethically easier, I think, because in them you have the suffering of the person who is experiencing something, and the continued treatment is continued suffering. When that is the case the reasoning behind forgoing life-sustaining treatment seems to be more compelling. But in the persistent vegetative state or permanent vegetative state, if the doctors are right, there is no awareness there, hence no suffering. Therefore some people ask, "If she's not suffering, what's the problem with keeping her alive? She doesn't feel anything, she isn't aware of what's being done to her."

At this point the conversation can go one of three ways. It can take up financial costs—which medical expenses are reasonable and which are wasteful. Or it can turn to the interests and needs of those close to the patient, such as the Schindlers and Mr. Schiavo, and focus on their interests and rights. Or it can turn to things owed to Terri that survive her permanent loss of consciousness and to what symbols and messages are healthy and appropriate for our society. All three are important to explore, but I believe we particularly need to concentrate our thinking on the last of these. What does it mean to honor a person's dignity, to respect their wishes and to honor their memory, even though they no longer have an identity or a presence in the form of consciousness? I think that's where we ethicists need to do more hard work. It's key to understanding what should be done in these cases, but it is difficult.

How Society Handled the Conflict

Finally, the reason I consider this case to be a "private tragedy," and a "public danger," is there is a still more general and important level of the controversy. It is a level at which this case tells us something, not about Terri Schiavo and PVS and families and medical ethics, but about ourselves as a society.

How well do we handle this kind of controversy, what kind of discourse we bring to bear on it? The law worked well in this case in the end, although it allowed matters to be drawn out for a very long time. But our politics failed. Our discourse largely failed. What, following the great philosopher John Dewey, we might call our "social intelligence" failed. That should trouble us and give us pause, as much as the long dying of an unfortunate young woman or the bitterness and heart break suffered by her family.

This is a case that is marked ... by the disagreements in our society between secular and religious perspectives. It is a case in which there is a striking discrepancy between the behavior of the executive and the legislative branches of our government and the judicial branch. The U.S. Congress pulled out all rhetorical stops in a midnight session. The president flew dramatically back from Texas and entered Washington on Palm Sunday. It was an extraordinary moment of political theater.

A short time later, the federal courts, with almost a shrug, said, "Are you kidding? What is the issue here? It's clear who should have the right to decide." The courts had a framework. And they used it, and they stuck to it, and it was not a particularly difficult decision for them. After all, the courts are guided largely by precedent and they had over one hundred such cases to pave the way in this decision.

Politicians, the elected officials, lack that kind of ethical, political agreement and framework that the courts enjoy. And so do we citizens in our general civic and moral culture. For us it was a terribly wrenching political matter. It's very important for elected officials, political leaders, to learn how to handle this sort of thing in a more reasoned, sober, and mature fashion. But it's no less important for citizens to learn how to handle these things in our own minds and hearts, in our own churches, communities, and conversations; so that we give the right message to our leaders who will then be reassured that we will support them if they act responsibly and judiciously, and that we will hold them accountable if they don't.

Questions Beyond Bioethics

At bottom the Schiavo case takes us from bioethics to questions of much larger scope. These are questions of toleration, compromise, of civic discourse itself. Can we compromise, or is this (feeding tubes, say) nonnegotiable? People take it at a very deep and fundamental values level. They take it at a very deep religious level. Yet we do need to learn to live together in peace, and that requires compromise.

One final thought on the perfect storm of controversy. To our shame, we lost sight of Terri Schiavo as a person, of her as a human being, regardless of the impairment, regardless of how close to death she might have been. We lost sight of her as a person and made her an icon. I submit that it's always dangerous and dehumanizing when that happens. And that worries me as much as anything else that we can talk about. This ceased to be about a human being who was dying; it became about an abstract symbol. It became about winning and losing. I hope and believe that most of the people who got caught up in that level of the discourse will soon look back at what they said and be ashamed of themselves, especially those who spoke so stridently and with too much confidence and too little humility in the media and on the Senate and House floors.

Looking Toward the Future

Let me conclude, not in a spirit of accusation and 20-20 hindsight, but by looking forward. Our end-of-life care legal framework did work, albeit slowly and painfully, in the Schiavo case. But it is not perfect, and we can do better in the future if we are able to stop circling the wagons and take a hard look at what still needs work.

To begin with, I think we have to take very seriously the idea that this framework is too individualistic and too adversarial. We need to figure out how to handle end of life decisions in other ways that do not put such a burden on people to navigate their own decisionmaking. Hospice does that very well. But a lot of people don't get into the hospice system, and they have to work through a very complicated system—a virtual minefield of medically aggressive and largely futile overtreatment—as they die.

Another major thing is, we have to take very seriously the possibility of various kinds of bias that have crept into our legal framework and our ethical framework. We do have to take seriously those who feel very much affronted by the idea that artificial nutrition and hydration could be withdrawn from a dying person. It is vital to resist this position, but not to dismiss it. The values and traditions behind it should be treated with serious engagement and respect. Here increasing scientific and medical understanding of how providing artificial nutrition and hydration can actually increase a patient's suffering (not comfort him) and actually shorten a person's life (not lengthen it), can allow us to remain firm in our grasp of the moral imperative of comfort and nurturance and remaining present to the dying while at the same time better under-standing how certain technologies actually work at cross pur-poses with that imperative. Common ground can be found.

Bias Against Disabled Persons

Moreover, we must take very seriously the perspective of those fellow citizens who live with impairments, who feel that there is a disvaluing of disabled life that has crept into this frame-work of autonomy in decisionmaking at the end of life. This, they argue, unduly biases decisionmaking against persons with functional limitations, as if their lives were somehow not worth preserving. The law is being used as an excuse to get them out of sight, out of mind, and out of the way.

I don't believe that such a critique accurately or fairly ap-plies to the persistent vegetative state and to the Terri Schiavo case. But there are other conditions of disability and impair-ment where this warning against bias, and a misplaced norm of able-bodied health, does apply. We must be aware of our own blind spots. In the years ahead, every moment and every ounce of political and moral energy we spend talking about the right to remove or refuse life-sustaining treatment, ought to be balanced by an equal amount of time and advocacy on how to provide adequate supports and services to persons who have chronic illness and disability.

If we don't balance the equation in that fashion, we will be guilty of a profound bias in our thinking and in our health care system. For too long we have focused on sustaining mean-ing and quality of life (as well as respecting rights and honor-ing wishes) only at the very end of life, in the last few pages of our stories. In the coming aging society, and even now, we very much need to move that concern upstream. The same concern and respect that we have shown for those quite close to death should be shown as well for the chronically ill and those living with disabilities several years before their death.

Since [the case of Karen] Quinlan we have empowered patients and families in the making of medical decisions, and the Schiavo case largely vindicates and reaffirms that empowerment. But that will be a hollow advance if we do not also support them with good systems of palliative and hospice care. And not just at the time of their final trip to the hospital, or even in their last six months of life, but for as long as their illness or impairment forces them to adapt and change. Not curing everything or living forever, but living well in the face of change and adversity, for however long we are given: that to me is the best lesson we can learn from the long dying of Terri Schiavo.

New Knowledge About Levels of Unconsciousness May Affect Life Support Decisions

Joseph J. Fins

Joseph J. Fins is head of the Division of Medical Ethics at Weill Medical College of Cornell University where he serves as a professor of medicine, a professor of public health, and a professor of medicine in psychiatry. *In the following selection, Fins explains that decisions about whether to withdraw life-sustaining treatment from brain-damaged patients are more difficult than in the past because of advances in neurology. Technologies such as MRI (magnetic resonance imaging) and PET (positron emission tomography) scans make it possible to differentiate disorders of consciousness more precisely than was formerly possible. It is now known that patients in a vegetative state sometimes progress to a minimally conscious state (MCS) before the vegetative state becomes permanent. However, the diagnosis of MCS is difficult and errors often occur. Fins points out that this can lead to inappropriate treatment if someone minimally conscious is labeled vegetative, or if someone who has been truly vegetative for a long time is thought to have minimal consciousness.*

Over the past several years, deciding whether to withdraw life-sustaining therapy from patients who have sustained severe brain injuries has become much more difficult. The problem is not the religious fundamentalism that infused the debate over the care of Terri Schiavo, the Florida woman in a permanent vegetative state whose case has drawn national attention. Rather, the difficulty stems from emerging knowledge about the diagnosis and physiology of brain injury and recov-

Joseph J. Fins, "Rethinking Disorders of Consciousness: New Research and Its Implications," *Hastings Center Report*, vol. 35, March–April 2005, pp. 22–24. Copyright © 2005 Hastings Center. Reproduced by permission.

ery. The advent of more sophisticated neuroimaging techniques like MRI and PET scans, in tandem with electrophysiologic and observational studies of brain-injured patients, have led to an effort to differentiate disorders of consciousness more precisely. The crude categories that have informed clinical practice for a quarter century are becoming obsolete.

It used to be enough for a neurologist or neurosurgeon to write a note in the chart grimly recording the patient's neurological exam and then concluding with the global statement, "no hope for meaningful recovery." It can no longer be so simple. With a better understanding of brain injury and mechanisms of recovery, we should be suspicious of blanket statements that might, we now believe, obscure important differences among different patients' prospects for recovery, although even those patients we now think may recover may still be left with profound and perhaps intolerable burdens of disability.

Recovery from coma depends on a patient's age, the site of injury, and whether the damage was done by trauma, anoxia (oxygen deprivation), or other processes. The most severe brain injuries may lead to brain death. If patients survive and begin to recover from coma, they often first enter into the vegetative state, first described by Bryan Jennett and my teacher, Fred Plum, in 1972. The vegetative state is a paradoxical state of "wakeful unresponsiveness" in which the eyes are open but there is no awareness of self or environment. When a vegetative state continues beyond thirty days, it is described as "persistent." A vegetative state is generally considered permanent three months after anoxic injury and twelve months after trauma.

Vegetative State Is Not Always Permanent

All of this is news since I went to medical school. I was taught that the vegetative state was immutable and fixed. Vegetative brains were, if I recall the phrase correctly, "gelatinous gels."

The futility of this brain state was the basis for the establishment of the right to die in cases like [those of Karen] *Quinlan* and [Nancy] *Cruzan*. Recent studies have shown, however, that patients can regain some evidence of consciousness before the vegetative state becomes permanent. In the window between the persistent and permanent vegetative state, patients can progress to what has been described as the "minimally conscious state" (MCS). Unlike vegetative patients, the minimally conscious demonstrate unequivocal, but fluctuating, evidence of awareness of self and the environment. The natural history of MCS patients is not yet known. Near the upper boundary of this category, patients may say words or phrases and gesture. They also may show evidence of memory, attention, and intention. Patients are considered to have "emerged" from MCS only when they can reliably and consistently communicate.

Unfortunately, all of this is easier to explain in theory than to observe in practice. First and foremost is the challenge of diagnosis. To the untrained eye, MCS patients may appear very similar to those who are vegetative. These diagnoses can be confused and conflated and in the earlier phases of illness need to be considered very carefully in the context of the mechanism of injury. In a patient with non-anoxic injury, even small gains beyond the vegetative level may herald the potential for significant further recovery. Some recent studies suggest that the diagnostic distinction between MCS and PVS is missed by neurologists at rates that would be intolerable in other clinical domains. To be fair, however, a neurologist acting in good faith might examine an MCS patient when his level of arousal was low and elicit an exam that is indistinguishable from a vegetative patient.

Value Judgments Can Affect Diagnosis

But there is another sort of diagnostic error that occurs when the objectivity of diagnosis is infiltrated by value judgments.

Instead of dealing with the moral ambiguity associated with balancing the burdens and possible benefits of continuing care, there is a tendency among some practitioners to act paternalistically and label some who might be minimally conscious as vegetative. By being categorical, the more difficult choices are side-stepped and the morass of the minimally conscious state is avoided. With "no hope for meaningful recovery," care can be withdrawn. But even if this is true—and it may be, since a patient in a minimally conscious state may indeed have no hope for meaningful recovery—our greater level of knowledge about these conditions calls for more diagnostic clarity.

Diagnostic distortion has also been used to undermine the right to die. In *Schiavo*, right to life advocates asserted that she was not vegetative. By suggesting consciousness where there was none, these opponents of choice at the end of life cast doubt on the ethical propriety of removing life-sustaining therapy. They persisted even though court-appointed physicians found that she was vegetative, and even when the Florida Supreme Court determined that there was clear and convincing evidence for this diagnosis.

A third sort of diagnostic distortion is journalistic. Differing brain states can be conflated either through ignorance of the facts or deliberately—to hype a case or new scientific development. . . .

Each of these distortions is troubling. If a distortion is a physician's it undermines the integrity of the clinical transaction. If it is inspired by ideology it politicizes a process that is better left to scientific judgment. And if it occurs through journalistic hubris, it perpetuates misunderstanding in the popular culture.

Balancing Slim Hopes Against Burdens

Families will have more than enough difficulty contending with disorders of consciousness even when they are properly diagnosed. Assuming that families can ascertain a credible diagnosis and prognosis, how should they make decisions about care? How should a slim prospect of recovering consciousness be balanced against the burdens associated with enduring disability? The protracted time frame during which recovery *might* occur could require a vigil that lasts for months and still might lead only to disappointment.

A long vigil may also preclude options to withdraw life-sustaining therapy. Consider the implications of the recent Papal statement on the ethical mandate to provide artificial nutrition and hydration to vegetative patients. If an observant Catholic family were to follow Church teachings, they might be able to discontinue "extraordinary" measures early in the patient's course when the prognosis was still unknown, but they might not be able to discontinue artificial nutrition and hydration later on, once it was clear that the patient would not make any progress from the vegetative state. This might cause some families to be more risk-aversive and withdraw extraordinary measures earlier in the course of illness while treatments like ventilators were still in place. The paradox is striking: A Papal statement intended to promote life might have the unintended consequence of limiting the chance of recovery for some.

To make matters even more complicated, these decisions will likely take place beyond the reach of the hospital and the expertise that is available in clinical ethics and neurology. Transfers out of the acute care setting can lead to errors of diagnostic omission and a failure to follow patients longitudinally as their condition evolves.

Misdiagnosis Leads to Tragedy

Such was the fate of Terry Wallis, an Arkansan who suffered traumatic brain injury in 1984 after a car accident. After he was diagnosed as being in a vegetative state, he was discharged to a nursing home, where he lingered for nineteen years. Although his family saw evidence of awareness, he did not receive an examination by a neurologist and never underwent an imaging study. His family was told that a work-up would be too expensive. The implication was that it was also pointless.

His case gained national press coverage in July 2003 when he began to speak. Headlines suggested that he had miraculously emerged from a coma. A closer examination of the record reveals that he had probably moved from the vegetative state to the minimally conscious state within the first months after his injury and then remained improperly diagnosed for years.

Stories like these send a chill up my spine. Some patients diagnosed as vegetative are probably in fact intermittently sentient but unable to communicate. The isolation, abandonment, and neglect they experience is unimaginable. Though their numbers may be small—there is no reliable data on how common this phenomenon is—they still make a claim of justice on all of us who know that some conscious but noncommunicative individuals may have been relegated to the margins of the human community. And they are but a small segment of a larger group of institutionalized patients with severe brain injuries who are receiving what has been described as merely "custodial care."

All of these patients deserve better. The small community of neuroscientists who have taken an interest in mechanisms of brain injury and recovery needs to be expanded, and bioethicists need to grapple with the imponderables, both theoretical and practical, that attend to disorders of consciousness. There is no shortage of questions about the nature of the self, personal identity, and autonomy to occupy us. Colloquially put, how much of yourself do you have to lose to cease to be you? The implications for an ethic grounded in self-determination are obvious and ripe for engagement by both theoretical and practical ethicists. . . .

If we hope to help patients and families make the tough choices following brain injury, we will need to embrace the ambiguity that goes along with long courses of recovery and questions about altered selves. These decisions will be more challenging than decisions to remove life support in the face of overwhelming sepsis or pursue treatment in the face of widely metastatic cancer. We will also need to demand diagnostic honesty and precision. In discussing diagnoses with families we will need to strike a balance between realism and hope. The objective must be to bring greater attention to the minimally conscious patient without engendering expectations for the permanently unconscious. If we are successful, we will protect both the right to die and the right to care, as paradoxical as that may seem in today's clinical and political climate.

CONTEMPORARY
ISSUES
COMPANION

CHAPTER 3

Physician-Assisted Suicide

Physician-Assisted Suicide Should Be Legal

Marcia Angell

Marcia Angell is a physician and the former editor-in-chief of the New England Journal of Medicine. *She now teaches at Harvard Medical School. In the following selection she explains her belief that physician-assisted suicide should be made available to dying patients. She states that although the treatment of pain at the end of life has improved greatly in recent years, it is still inadequate and that symptoms other than pain during terminal illness are often harder to manage. In Angell's opinion, the suffering of protracted death is completely pointless. Although she recognizes that advocates of palliative care disagree, she argues that not all patients have the same attitude toward death. She asserts that those who wish to hasten death should be given that choice.*

Death is not fair and it is often cruel. Some die young, others in extreme old age. Some die quickly, others slowly but peacefully. Some find personal or religious meaning in the process, as well as an opportunity, for a final reconciliation with loved ones. Others, especially those with cancer, AIDS, or progressive neurologic disorders, die by inches and in great anguish. Good palliative care usually can help in these cases, but not always and often not enough. The problem is not just pain, although that can be devastating. Other symptoms, such as breathlessness and nausea, can be worse and even harder to relieve. There are no good treatments for weakness, loss of bodily functions, and helplessness—probably the most important reasons for despair in those who are dying slowly, along with the knowledge that it can only grow worse.

Just as dying differs, so too do people's hopes and fears about their own deaths. Most people probably hope for a sudden death—in old age during sleep—but not everyone. Some would prefer a slower death, to have time to prepare and to take leave of loved ones. For some, the ultimate terror is loss of their mental faculties. For others, it is intractable pain, and for still others, it is immobility, dependence, and a loss of control over the circumstances of their lives. Experience in Oregon in the six years since its Death with Dignity Act came into effect is illuminating. Under this act, patients with terminal illness may request physicians to help them hasten death by providing a prescription for a lethal dose of sleeping pills. Physicians may legally do so, if they choose, and the state has kept careful records of the practice. Those records show that fear of loss of control is a powerful motive for those who request help in ending their lives—or, more properly, in ending their protracted dying.

The Process of Dying

Like other healthy, young people, I knew little about death when I went to medical school forty years ago. . . . In those days, physicians and their instructors paid little formal attention to the dying process. I do not remember a single mention of it in the medical school curriculum. It was as though dying were a medical failure and thus too shameful to be discussed. As doctors, we were to succeed, not fail, and success was measured by our ability to stave off death. Our failures were kept hidden.

Sooner or later, of course, my classmates and I did come into contact with death—not the peaceful death of our fantasies but death as it really happened, over and over again, in the hospitals where we worked. Some deaths were peaceful, but we also saw patients in virtually unrelieved agony, often because pain medication was given in doses too small and too far apart. We saw patients isolated as they died—by their doctors because we thought there was nothing more we could do for them and by their families because we conspired with them to withhold the truth from dying patients. On morning hospital rounds, we simply avoided dying patients—this despite the fact that most of us went to medical school at least in part because we wanted to relieve suffering. Sometimes doctors—particularly the older, experienced ones—would hasten the deaths of suffering patients by administering large doses of morphine, but the practice was rarely explicitly acknowledged. All of this we young doctors were left to absorb silently. It had no place in the curriculum or in the discourse of the medical profession at large. We just did not talk about it.

The Importance of Treating Pain

I broke my own silence on the subject in 1982, a few years after I had joined the editorial staff of the *New England Journal of Medicine*. In an editorial entitled . . . "The Quality of Mercy," I criticized the systematic failure to treat pain adequately in dying patients. . . .

I ended the editorial with an appeal to doctors: "Pain is soul destroying. No patient should have to endure intense pain unnecessarily. The quality of mercy is essential to the practice of medicine; here, of all places, it should not be strained."

Since then, largely stimulated by the hospice movement that began in London and found widespread acceptance in the United States in the 1980s, attitudes toward the treatment of pain at the end of life have improved greatly. The use of patient-regulated intravenous pain relief is now common, providing the flexibility and control I advocated more than twenty years ago. New methods of treating pain have been devised, and pain clinics have been established in many medical centers and large hospitals. In addition, the whole spectrum of symptoms of dying patients is now receiving professional attention. Hospice care is widely available, and palliative medicine is a recognized specialty. Despite all this progress, however, pain relief is still generally inadequate, particularly for children and other vulnerable patients, and there are still exaggerated concerns about "drug-seeking" patients and the side effects of opiates.

Existential Suffering

Symptoms of terminal illness other than pain are often harder to manage. That is particularly true of existential suffering— the sense of the utter pointlessness of a protracted death. If tomorrow will be worse than today, one day after another until the end, why not die today? Why continue to disintegrate, to lose bodily functions, to grow ever more helpless and dependent? I believe it was largely because of such feelings that a movement arose to legalize physician-assisted suicide as a choice for the dying, even as the palliative care movement also grew in importance.

Over time I became convinced that physician-assisted suicide should be an option for dying patients when palliative care has failed. I further came to believe that the judgment as to whether palliation had failed could be made only by each patient individually, since suffering is entirely subjective. My growing conviction was reinforced by my father's death [by suicide] in 1988. I told his story in an amicus brief on behalf of Oregon in *Oregon v. Ashcroft* (the U.S. attorney general's ongoing attempt to nullify the Oregon Death with Dignity Act) and in the *Washington Post....* [That story concluded:]

> My father's situation was hardly unique or even unusual. Many people with terminal illness face the same dilemma. It is not a choice between life and death. It is a choice between a slow, agonizing death and a quick, merciful one. Many people—not just my father—would choose the latter if they could. What was unusual about my father was not his choice, but his courage and resolve in achieving it. The Oregon

Death with Dignity Act makes that choice much easier for patients and their families. But it does not preclude people from making a different choice. People who prefer a longer life to an easier death are not prevented from choosing that. It seems to me that Oregon has chosen a path that gives dying patients the opportunity to exercise the greatest possible self-determination with the full support of their families and communities. I cannot imagine why anyone would want to prevent that.

Trusting Dying Patients

Ironically, some of the people who *do* want to prevent that are closely associated with the move to improve palliative care, including advocates of good hospice care. An unfortunate schism has opened up between people who have in common the overarching desire to mitigate suffering at the end of life. In a recent book, *The Case against Assisted Suicide*, edited by Kathleen Foley and Herbert Hendin, some of the most prominent opponents of physician-assisted suicide argue their case. The arguments vary. For some, it is a moral matter, although it is hard for me to imagine anything morally uplifting about requiring helpless people to endure protracted agony. [Leon] Kass states, "Doctors must not kill." But physician-assisted suicide is not about "'killing"; rather, it is about helping patients to hasten their own deaths. And surely there is something off point in Kass's focus on doctors, not patients. Other essayists emphasize medical considerations rather than moral ones. To them, assisted suicide is not necessary. They believe that all suffering can be relieved if caregivers are sufficiently skillful and compassionate. They fear that permitting physician-assisted suicide would deflect attention from providing good palliative care.

I have no doubt that if expert palliative care were available to everyone who needed it, there would be few requests for assisted suicide. I also have no doubt that even under the best of circumstances, there will always be a few patients whose suffering simply cannot be adequately alleviated; and there will be some who would prefer suicide to other measures to deal with unremitting suffering, such as heavy sedation without fluids and food until death. I would like to be proved wrong about this. I would welcome all attempts to show that palliative care can be so effective that no one wants physician-assisted suicide. That outcome could only be achieved, however, by preserving the choice, not closing it off. It would require trust that dying patients know what they want. If physician-assisted suicide is illegal, there will be no way of knowing whether . . . the hospice and palliative care movement has been successful—whether it has won its point and physician-assisted suicide is truly unnecessary. We cannot simply assume that good palliative care is always effective.

I am also concerned that the hospice and palliative care movement, as it has grown in importance and influence, has developed a mindset typical of many specialized disciplines: a professional pride that borders on hubris and rigidity. Proponents have in some respects devised a picture of a good death that is no less stylized than the one I brought to medical school. In this picture, patients see the dying process as a time of "growth," during which they come to realize deeper meanings in their lives and relationships and eventually achieve a peaceful acceptance of death. Suffering is to some extent overcome by this acceptance. As [British hospice founder C.A.] Saunders puts it, "People need time to evaluate their lives, repair their relationships, and plan for others. They may also find new depth of enjoyment in a transient world."

This ideal of the good death does not leave much room for patients for whom control and independence are highly important—people like my father, people who dread dying more than they fear death. I have even heard such people disparaged as overly controlling—as though they should somehow get with the program and die right. But it is wrong to assume that all people will approach death the same way. Some will, indeed, become ideal hospice patients, but others will rail against the dying process until the end, and they will want that end to come sooner. They too are human. We should be careful not to impose our views of a good death on others.

Assisted Suicide Is a Matter of Mercy

Long before my father's death, I believed that physician-assisted suicide ought to be permissible under some circumstances, but his death strengthened my conviction that it is simply a part of good medical care, something to be provided reluctantly and sadly, as a last resort, but provided nonetheless. There should be safeguards to ensure that the decision is well considered and consistent, but these should not be so daunting or so violate privacy that they become obstacles instead of protections. In particular, they should be directed not toward reviewing the reasons for an autonomous decision but only toward ensuring that the decision is indeed autonomous.

There is no right way to die, and there should be no schism between advocates for better palliative care and advocates for making the choice of assisted suicide available. Surely every effort should be made to improve palliative care, as I argued in 1982. When those efforts are unavailing and suffering patients desperately long to end their lives, they should have the choice to do so. The argument that permitting physician-assisted suicide would deflect us from redoubling our commitment to good palliative care asks these patients to pay the penalty for our failings. It is also illogical. Good palliative care and the availability of physician-assisted suicide are no more mutually exclusive than good cardiologic care and the availability of heart transplantation. To require dying patients to endure unrelievable suffering, regardless of their wishes, is callous and unseemly. Death is hard enough without being bullied. Like the relief of pain, this too is a matter of mercy.

Physician-Assisted Suicide Should Not Be Legal

Marilyn Golden

Marilyn Golden is a policy analyst at the Disability Rights Education and Defense Fund (DREDF), a national law and policy center on disability civil rights. In the following selection she argues that although assisted suicide might help a few people, it would harm many. Profit-driven managed health care and assisted suicide are "a deadly mix," Golden says, because it is much cheaper to encourage people to die than to provide care for them. She also states that fear of, and prejudice against, disability is a major factor in the support for legalization of assisted suicide. In addition, she points out that many external pressures might lead to decisions to die, so that the free choice alleged to be offered by legalization of assisted suicide would inevitably result in deaths due to lack of choice. Therefore, in Golden's opinion, the practice should remain illegal.

Assisted suicide seems, at first blush, like a good thing to have available. But on closer inspection, there are many reasons legalization is a very serious mistake. Supporters often focus solely on superficial issues of choice and self-determination. It is crucial to look deeper.

We must separate our private wishes for what we each may hope to have available for ourselves some day and, rather, focus on the significant dangers of legalizing assisted suicide as public policy in this society as it operates today. Assisted suicide would have many unintended consequences.

A Very Few Helped—A Great Many Harmed

The movement for legalization of assisted suicide is driven by anecdotes of people who suffer greatly in the period before

Marilyn Golden, "Why Assisted Suicide Must Not Be Legalized," *Disability Rights Education and Defense Fund*, October 6, 2004. Reproduced by permission.

death. But the overwhelming majority of these anecdotes describes either situations for which legal alternatives exist today, or situations in which the individual would not be legally eligible for assisted suicide. It is legal in every U.S. state for an individual to create an advance directive that requires the withdrawal of treatment under any conditions the person wishes. It is legal for a patient to refuse any treatment or to require any treatment to be withdrawn. It is legal to receive sufficient painkillers to be comfortable, even if they might hasten death. And if someone who is imminently dying is in significant discomfort, it is legal for the individual to be sedated to the point that the discomfort is relieved. Moreover, if someone has a chronic illness that is not terminal, that individual is not eligible for assisted suicide under any proposal in the U.S., nor under the Oregon Death with Dignity Act (Oregon is the only state where assisted suicide is legal). Furthermore, any individual whose illness has brought about depression that affects the individual's judgment is also ineligible, according to every U.S. proposal as well as Oregon's law. Consequently, the number of people whose situations would actually be eligible for assisted suicide is extremely low.

The very small number of people who may benefit from legalizing assisted suicide will tend to be affluent, white, and in possession of good health insurance coverage. At the same time, large numbers of people, particularly among those less privileged in society, would be at significant risk of harm.

Managed Care and Assisted Suicide— A Deadly Mix

Perhaps the most significant problem is the deadly mix between assisted suicide and profit-driven managed health care. Again and again, health maintenance organizations (HMOs) and managed care bureaucracies have overruled physicians' treatment decisions. These actions have sometimes hastened patients' deaths. The cost of the lethal medication generally used for assisted suicide is about $35 to $50, far cheaper than the cost of treatment for most long-term medical conditions. The incentive to save money by denying treatment already poses a significant danger. This danger would be far greater if assisted suicide is legal.

Assisted suicide is likely to accelerate the decline in quality of our health care system. A 1998 study from Georgetown University's Center for Clinical Bioethics underscores the link between profit-driven managed health care and assisted suicide. The research found a strong link between cost-cutting pressure on physicians and their willingness to prescribe lethal drugs to patients, were it legal to do so. The study warns that there must be "a sobering degree of caution in legalizing [assisted suicide] in a medical care environment that is characterized by increasing pressure on physicians to control the cost of care."

The deadly impact of legalizing assisted suicide would fall hardest on socially and economically disadvantaged people who have less access to medical resources and who already find themselves discriminated against by the health care system. As Paul Longmore, Professor of History at San Francisco State University and a foremost disability advocate on this subject, has stated, "Poor people, people of color, elderly people, people with chronic or progressive conditions or disabilities, and anyone who is, in fact, terminally ill will find themselves at serious risk." . . .

Supporters of assisted suicide frequently say that HMOs will not use this procedure as a way to deal with costly patients. They cite a 1998 study in the *New England Journal of Medicine* that estimated the savings of allowing people to die before their last month of life at $627 million. Supporters argue that this is a mere .07% of the nation's total annual health care costs. But significant problems in this study make it an unsuitable basis for claims about assisted suicide's potential impact. The researchers based their findings on the average cost to Medicare of patients with only four weeks or less to live. Yet assisted suicide proposals (as well as the law in Oregon) define terminal illness as having *six months* to live. The researchers also assumed that about 2.7% of the total number of people who die in the U.S. would opt for assisted suicide, based on reported assisted suicide and euthanasia deaths in the Netherlands. But the failure of large numbers of Dutch physicians to report such deaths casts considerable doubt on this estimate. And how can one compare the U.S. to a country that has universal health care? Taken together, these factors would skew the costs much higher.

Fear, Bias, and Prejudice Against Disability

Fear, bias, and prejudice against disability play a significant role in assisted suicide. Who ends up using assisted suicide? Supporters advocate its legalization by arguing that it would relieve untreated pain and discomfort at the end of life. But *all but one* of the people in Oregon who were reported to have used that state's assisted suicide law during its first year wanted suicide *not* because of pain, but for fear of losing functional ability, autonomy, or control of bodily functions (Oregon Health Division, 1999). Oregon's subsequent reports have documented similar results. Furthermore, in the Netherlands, more than half the physicians surveyed say the main reason given by patients for seeking death is "loss of dignity."

This fear of disability typically underlies assisted suicide. Said one assisted suicide advocate, "Pain is not the main reason we want to die. It's the indignity. It's the inability to get out of bed or get onto the toilet . . . [People] . . . say, 'I can't stand my mother—my husband—wiping my behind.' It's about dignity." But as many thousands of people with disabilities who rely on personal assistance have learned, needing help is not undignified, and death is not better than reliance on assistance. Have we gotten to the point that we will abet suicides because people need help using the toilet?

Diane Coleman, President and Founder of Not Dead Yet, a grassroots disability organization opposed to legalizing assisted suicide, has written that the "public image of severe disability as a fate worse than death ... become(s) grounds for carving out a deadly exception to longstanding laws and public policies about suicide intervention services.... Legalizing assisted suicide means that some people who say they want to die will receive suicide intervention, while others will receive suicide assistance. The difference between these two groups of people will be their health or disability status, leading to a two-tiered system that results in death to the socially devalued group."

Undiagnosed Depression Underlies Requests for Assisted Suicide

Suicide requests from people with terminal illness are usually based on fear and depression. As Herbert Hendin, M.D., Medical Director of the American Foundation for Suicide Prevention and a leading U.S. expert on suicide, stated in Congressional testimony in 1996, "a request for assisted suicide is ... usually made with as much ambivalence as are most suicide attempts. If the doctor does not recognize that ambivalence as well as the anxiety and depression that underlie the patient's request for death, the patient may become trapped by that request and die in a state of unrecognized terror."

Most cases of depression among terminally ill people can be successfully treated. Yet primary care physicians are generally not experts in diagnosing depression. Where assisted suicide is legalized, the depression remains undiagnosed, and the only treatment consists of a lethal prescription.

Assisted suicide proposals and Oregon's law are based on the faulty assumption that it is possible to make a clear distinction between those who are terminally ill with six months to live, and everyone else. Everyone else is supposedly protected and not eligible for assisted suicide. But it is extremely common for medical prognoses of a short life expectancy to be wrong. Studies show that only cancer patients show a predictable decline, and even then, it's only in the last few weeks of life. With every disease other than cancer, there is no predictability at all. Prognoses are based on statistical averages, which are nearly useless in predicting what will happen to an individual patient. Thus, the potential effect of assisted suicide is extremely broad, far beyond the supposedly narrow group its proponents claim. The affected group could include many people who may be mistakenly diagnosed as terminal but who have many meaningful years of life ahead of them.

This also poses considerable danger to people with new or progressive disabilities or diseases. Research overwhelmingly shows that people with new disabilities frequently go through initial despondency and suicidal feelings, but later adapt well and find great satisfaction in their lives. However, the adaptation usually takes considerably longer than the mere two week waiting period required by assisted suicide proposals and Oregon's law. People with new diagnoses of terminal illness appear to go through similar stages. In that early period before one learns the truth about how good one's quality of life can be, it would be all too easy, if assisted suicide is legal, to make the final choice, one that is irrevocable.

Supposed Safeguards Are Illusory

Neither do other alleged safeguards offer any real protections. In Oregon's law and similar proposals, physicians are not permitted to write a lethal prescription under inappropriate conditions that are defined in the law. This is seen as a "safeguard." But in several Oregon cases, suicidal patients engaged in "doctor shopping." When the first physician each of these patients approached refused to comply with the request for assisted suicide because the patient didn't meet the conditions of the law, the patient sought out another physician who agreed. The compliant physicians were often assisted suicide advocates. Such was the case of Kate Cheney, age 85, as described in the *Oregonian* in October 1999. Her physician refused to prescribe lethal medication, because he thought the request, rather than being Ms. Cheney's free choice, actually resulted from pressure by her assertive daughter who felt burdened with care giving. So the family found another doctor, and Ms. Cheney soon used the prescribed drugs and died.

Another purported safeguard is that physicians are required to discuss alternatives to assisted suicide. However, there is no requirement that these alternatives be made available. Kate Cheney's case exemplifies this. Further, the Kate Cheney case demonstrates the shocking laxness with which safeguards in Oregon are being followed. Ms. Cheney decided to take the lethal medication after spending just a week in a nursing home, to give her family a break from caretaking. The chronology shows that Cheney felt she had only three choices: burdening her family, the hell of a nursing home, or death. . . .

So-called "Narrow" Proposals Will Inevitably Expand

Proponents claim that assisted suicide will be narrowly limited to those who are terminally ill, but these so-called "narrow" proposals will inevitably be expanded. . . . The longest experience we have with assisted suicide is in the Netherlands, where active euthanasia as well as assisted suicide are practiced. The Netherlands has become a frightening laboratory experiment because assisted suicide and euthanasia have meant that "pressure for improved palliative care appears to have evaporated," according to Herbert Hendin, M.D., in his Congressional testimony in 1996. Hendin was one of only three foreign observers given the opportunity to study these medical practices in the Netherlands in depth, to discuss specific cases with leading practitioners, and to interview Dutch government-sponsored euthanasia researchers. He documented how assisted suicide and euthanasia have become not the rare exception, but the rule for people with terminal illness in the Netherlands.

"Over the past two decades," Hendin continued, "the Netherlands has moved from assisted suicide to euthanasia, from euthanasia for the terminally ill to euthanasia for the chronically ill, from euthanasia for physical illness to euthanasia for psychological distress and from voluntary euthanasia to nonvoluntary and involuntary euthanasia. Once the Dutch accepted assisted suicide it was not possible legally or morally to deny more active medical (assistance to die), i.e. euthanasia, to those who could not effect their own deaths. Nor could they deny assisted suicide or euthanasia to the chronically ill who have longer to suffer than the terminally ill or to those who have psychological pain not associated with physical disease. To do so would be a form of discrimination. Involuntary euthanasia has been justified as necessitated by the need to make decisions for patients not [medically] competent to choose for themselves." Hendin describes how, for a substantial number of people in the Netherlands, physicians have ended their patients' lives without consultation with the patients. . . .

Claims of Free Choice Are Illusory

Assisted suicide purports to be about free choice and self-determination. But there is significant danger that many people would take this "escape" due to external pressure. For example, elderly individuals who don't want to be a financial or caretaking burden on their families might choose assisted death. In Oregon's third year Report, "a startling 63% of [reported cases] cited fear of being a 'burden on family, friends or caregivers' as a reason for their suicide."

Also very troubling, research has documented widespread elder abuse in this country. The perpetrators are often family members (National Elder Abuse Incidence Study, 1996). Such abuse could easily lead to pressures on elders to "choose" assisted suicide. . . .

Still others would undergo assisted suicide because they lack good health care, or in-home support, and are terrified about going to a nursing home. As Diane Coleman noted regarding Oregon's law, "Nor is there any requirement that sufficient home and community-based long-term care services be provided to relieve the demands on family members and ease the individual's feelings of being a 'burden' . . . . The inadequacy of the in-home long-term care system is central to the assisted suicide and euthanasia debate."

While the proponents of legalization argue that it would guarantee choice, assisted suicide would actually result in deaths due to a *lack* of choice. Real choice would require adequate home and community-based long-term care; universal health insurance; housing that is available, accessible, and affordable; and other social supports. In a perverse twist, widespread acceptance of assisted suicide is likely to *reduce* pressure on society to provide these very kinds of support services, thus reducing genuine options even further, just as Herbert Hendin observed that widespread use of euthanasia in the Netherlands has substantially decreased pressure there for improved palliative care, by decreasing demand for it.

As Paul Longmore has stated, "Given the absence of any real choice, death by assisted suicide becomes not an act of personal autonomy, but an act of desperation. It is fictional freedom; it is phony autonomy."

Refuting Arguments in Favor of Physician-Assisted Suicide

Kevin Yuill

Kevin Yuill teaches American history at the University of Sunderland in England. He has written many articles about end-of-life issues for Spiked, an online magazine. The following selection is one of these articles. In it, he refutes ten arguments that have commonly been used in support of assisted suicide. As Yuill points out, suicide is already legal; allowing physicians to assist gives more power to doctors than to patients. Furthermore, assisted suicide laws are opposed not only by religious groups, but by the disabled, who fear that social acceptance of suicide assistance for the seriously ill will imply that their own lives are not worth living. In Yuill's opinion, the desire for assisted death is motivated by fear. He believes that dignity comes not from choosing how to die, but from bearing up under suffering and from facing fears rather than caving into them.

It is worth picking apart some of the arguments for assisted suicide.

Who Has the Power?

1. This is just about individual autonomy. [In both Britain and the United States] individuals already have the right to commit suicide. Nobody today could be hanged for attempting suicide, as was the case in the nineteenth century—nor would they be imprisoned for their unsuccessful attempt.

[Legislation under consideration in Britain] would remove the penalty, ... for aiding a suicide. As the psychiatrist Thomas Szasz has pointed out, '(s)trictly speaking, assisted suicide is an oxymoron'. The only people who would be 'empowered' by this bill would be doctors, who would decide whether or not the patient is 'competent', certify that the patient's illness is 'terminal' and '[conclude] that the patient is suffering unbearably as a result of that terminal illness'.

2. We all need the 'right to die.' We all have the right to die, with or without its sanction in law. All the 'patients' of Dr Jack Kevorkian, currently in prison in America for having gone a little too far in assisting the suicide of Thomas Youk (which was videotaped and shown on CBS's *60 Minutes*), were physically capable of bringing about their own deaths.

Anyone, with a little forward planning and much determination, can kill themselves. The [bill being debated] will instead place an onus on doctors and carers to help individuals to commit suicide. One of the most ugly arguments to come from the Voluntary Euthanasia Society is that disabled people should have the right to die, too. We must be clear that we are being obligated to give the proverbial man on the bridge a push (or perhaps to make the bridge wheelchair accessible).

The Value of Life

3. Those opposing assisted suicide are a 'small religious minority.' It is true that many religious groups vehemently oppose [legalisation], but they are not the only ones. They unite with medical representatives and disabled groups, who fear that doctors' judgements about 'quality of life' may imply that their own lives are not worth living.

This is no abstract fear voiced by philosophers such as Baroness [Mary] Warnock, as Jane Campbell, writing recently in *The Times* (London), discovered. Campbell, who suffers from spinal muscular atrophy, a muscle-wasting illness that means she cannot lift her head from her pillow unaided, was hospitalised for a case of pneumonia. The consultant treating her said that he assumed she would not want to be resuscitated should she go into respiratory failure. When she protested that she would like to be resuscitated, she was visited by a more senior consultant who said that he assumed she would not want to be put on a ventilator. According to the Disability Rights Commission, this was not was not an isolated incident. As Campbell says, these incidents 'reflect society's view that people such as myself live flawed and unsustainable lives and that death is preferable to living with a severe impairment'.

In fact, it is those calling for legalisation of assisted suicide who tend to espouse New Age religious values. 'Self-deliverance' is the term favoured by Derek Humphry, . . . author of the best-selling suicide bible, *Final Exit*. Delivery to where, Mr. Humphry? Dr Timothy Quill, who admitted in an article in the *New England Journal of Medicine* that he had helped a patient die, has written a book called *A Midwife through the Dying Process*. To an atheist (like myself), death is not an 'experience' but the end of all experiences. Do assisted suicide advocates wish simply to replace rituals formerly carried out by priests?

Finally, you need not be Christian to agree with the Archbishop of Canterbury that 'the respect for human life in all its stages is the foundation of a civilised society'.

4. Allowing the right to die is the hallmark of a civilised society. To break the taboo against suicide would be a sure sign of societal breakdown. Though the disintegration of society and the disappearance of socially integrating institutions receive much attention, there is little recognition of the relationship with the right-to-die movement. The sociologist Emile Durkheim made the point that 'Man is the more vulnerable to self-destruction the more he is detached from any collectivity.' Is suicide not the most awful manifestation of the 'drop out' society? To encourage it is a celebration of alienation and anomie. The taboo on suicide marks the recognition of our interdependence. We should maintain it.

Even Mary Warnock pointed out, what sort of society tells its members that it values their right to starve to death, especially if they are a burden on society? Surely a mark of civilisation would be to offer people in despair some sort of argument that their lives *are* valuable, that they do have some worth. Instead, right-to-die advocates project their own gloomy estimation of the worth of human life on to these poor souls.

Pain and Dignity

5. The central issue is pain. Not according to any available study. In 1995, an update to the authoritative Remmelink Report on euthanasia in Holland, where the practice has long been accepted and is now legal, showed that pain played a role in only 32 percent of requests for euthanasia. In no case did pain represent the sole reason for requests. In Oregon, USA, under right-to-die legislation that is seen as a blueprint for [the British] bill, only 28 out of 129 physician-assisted deaths in the first five years cited pain as the most important factor (the primary reasons was fear of what the future might bring). The suffering occurring at the end of life is real enough, but it involves fears rather than simply physical pain.

6. This is all about 'dignity.' What sort of dignity? Right-to-die campaigners condemn the lives of the disabled as bereft of dignity, apparently associating dignity solely with control over bodily functions. According to this definition, if someone loses their bodily 'autonomy', they no longer have human dignity. In my mind, dignity comes from bearing up under suffering we meet throughout our lives rather than letting it destroy us, and from facing fears rather than caving in to them.

Fear of the Future

7. Many are forced into 'lonely, back-street suicides' because of our restrictive laws. The good news is that fewer people are actually committing suicide today.... Very few Britons become 'suicide tourists'. In six years, only 180 people took up the option of assisted suicide under Oregon's right-to-die law, which is less than one percent of those requesting information about it. Even in Holland, where assisted suicide has been legal for some time, the numbers are low. Prominent campaigners for the right to die such as [counterculture guru] Timothy Leary have backed out of suicide at the last minute. In most polls, those who are keenest advocates for legalising assisted suicide are the young. The elderly, whom one might imagine have most cause, tend to shun it.

The real power behind the right-to-die campaigns is fear. Imagine, campaigners say, if you were trapped, forced to live a life you no longer wanted, unable to end it yourself. But as Elisabeth Kubler-Ross, pioneering author of *On Death and Dying*, noted, the attraction of assisted suicide is really about the projection of present fears about life on to dying.

We must ask what a person is saying when they ask for assisted suicide. If an individual was determined to die, they would hatch a plan and tell nobody about it. By asking for an assisted suicide, an individual is expressing their despair about their prospects, their fear for what the future holds. Why would they express despair unless they wanted some sort of connection with others? Why would someone with a true wish to alienate themselves from human contact forever tell someone about it? We ill serve those who express hopelessness by agreeing with them and, worse, cheering them on.

8. *Allowing assisted suicide would restore a right enjoyed by classical societies.* In fact, approving of suicide as a therapy would be unprecedented in human history. Assisted suicide advocates often justify their beliefs by invoking ancient societies, especially Athens, where apparently rationality reigned and suicide was tolerated. Yet in fact, at that time suicides were buried away from other graves; the suicide's self-murdering hand was cut off and buried apart. Ancient Greeks and Romans often took their own lives for reasons of grief, high patriotic principle, or to avoid dishonor, but these deaths gained meaning by emphasising societal values. Plato allowed that suicide might be permitted for reasons of painful disease or intolerable restraint, but he argued that the subject had first to plead their case before the Senate.

The solipsism of today's suicide advocates stands out. Suicide for the reason that an individual's life is wretched puts aside relationships with others. It ignores the union between the dead, the living, and the as yet unborn. To throw away a life for such paltry reasons mocks those who, in the past, sacrificed themselves to extend and enrich life, and risks demoralising those who are just entering our world.

However, one precedent for a tolerant view of suicide exists. Germany between the years of 1900–1945 presupposed many of the ideas of the assisted suicide movement. Depends on your view of 'classical', I guess.

The Illusion of a Good Death

9. The real problem is modern technology's ability to keep people alive indefinitely. Did someone invent a cure for death that I didn't hear about? The blurb on one book notes: 'As medical technology advances to the point when any human life can be maintained almost indefinitely, questions related to the "quality" of that life inevitably arise.' It is instructive that the authors chose not to celebrate the triumph of medical science but to look for potential problems.

10. It is best to die as you choose, surrounded by friends and relatives at home rather than by tubes and monitors in a hospital. We cannot control when and how we die; to give the 'right' to do so is as meaningful as giving people the right not to die of heart attacks or accidents. The holistic, back-to-nature view, apparent in many medical ethics books, imagines that we have become alienated from death and over-reliant on trying to extend life by technological means. It is understandable that many people would prefer to die away from a hospital, but the search for a 'good death' will forever prove elusive. Every death is ugly and undignified, as life is wrenched away, leaving an inanimate, waxen corpse. Those who seek the security of a good death seek to inure themselves to uncertainty, perhaps because they have witnessed the prolonged death of a close relative or friend. But this is a projection of our own technophobic fears on to the dying person.

So shall we project our own cramped and gloomy worldview on to those who are most sensitive to counsels of despair? Or shall we continue to view all human life as valuable, doctors as curers of physical disease (rather than prescribers of death for therapeutic reasons), and life as worth living?

Disabled People Disagree About Physician-Assisted Suicide

Barry Corbet

Barry Corbet was a member of the first American team to climb Mt. Everest. A few years after that accomplishment, however, he suffered a spinal cord injury in a helicopter crash, and from then until his death in 2004, was confined to a wheelchair. He was the editor of New Mobility *for many years. In the following selection he discusses the views of disabled people toward physician-assisted death. Almost all disability rights organizations are strongly opposed to all forms of it. However, Corbet states that while the leadership of these groups presumes to speak for the members, more than half of the people with disabilities polled nationwide support physician-assisted suicide and many of them fear criticism if they speak out in favor of it. In addition, organizations that offer information and counseling to people who want to kill themselves without the assistance of doctors provide an alternative to assisted suicide laws. In Corbet's opinion, this may be preferable to implementing assisted suicide in a flawed health-care system that would be open to systematic abuse.*

It's so deceptive, this one simple question: Should we make it legal for people to secure a doctor's assistance in hastening death? Yes or no? Ask, and you might get a definitive answer. Ask why, and what you'll get is slippery, contentious, anything but definitive. . . .

The discord begins with a name—whatever we're going to call death requested by a patient and facilitated by a physician. The most commonly used term is physician-assisted suicide, or PAS. In disability circles, that acronym stands for personal

Barry Corbet, "Physician Assisted Death: Are We Asking the Right Questions?" *New Mobility*, www.newmobility.com, May 2003. Reproduced by permission.

assistance services, so is rejected here. Not Dead Yet [NDY], a major player in the debate, prefers physician-induced death, or PID. It has undertones of medical murder so is rejected on the basis of bias. For this discussion, I've compromised with physician-assisted death, or PAD.

Some background: Suicide is legal in every state, as is passively attending a suicide. Euthanasia, actively helping someone end their life, is illegal in every state. PAD, a physician providing a lethal dose for a patient to take without further assistance, is legal only in Oregon.

Two disability rights-based organizations have formed to address the PAD question: Not Dead Yet, which opposes PAD and the Oregon law, and AUTONOMY, which endorses both. The Hemlock Society has been given much weight because it is the country's oldest and largest group supporting PAD and often incurs NDY's and AUTONOMY's wrath. . . .

As president of The Hemlock Society, Faye Girsh (now vice-president), asked me what seems like a reasonable question: "Why can't those who don't want hastened death live out their full lifespans and those who do want it have this humane option available to them?" Girsh meant the question innocently, but is it truly benign? Not if it's the alpha and omega of the discussion. It sweeps way too many valid concerns under the rug, even on a personal level. . . .

PAD as a Disability Issue

Here's another reasonable-sounding question, this time from the late [disability rights activist] Drew Batavia: "Disability rights are about autonomy and self-determination. Why shouldn't that freedom of choice extend to end-of-life decisions?"

Because, NDY might say, the current state of institutionalized prejudice against people with disabilities turns that choice into no choice. Because nondisabled people seem to fear disability more than death. Because doctors are fallible in diagnosing and treating depression and estimating life expectancy. Because the current rush to cut health-care costs conflicts with our need for lifelong care. Because PAD can be seen as the ultimate sanction, the ultimate form of discrimination.

Our PAD "choices" may, in fact, be subtly conditioned. "The problem is that our desires are so malleable and manipulable," says Harriet McBryde Johnson, a disability rights attorney from Charleston, S.C., and a supporter of NDY. "You know how easy it is to internalize other people's expectations, how exhausting it can be to oppose them, especially when you're sick. What we confront usually isn't homicidal hate, it's that pervasive assumption that our lives are inherently bad. That attitude can wear us down to the point where we want to be killed."

Can't we build ironclad safeguards into the law?

"Safeguards as presently proposed," counters Johnson, "are about defining a class whose desire to die may be presumed rational, because of illness or disability so 'bad' that no 'reasonable' person would want to endure it. That whole veneer of beneficence. The law has the power to validate and structure prejudice. These [PAD] laws tell suicidal newbies that yes, it really is as bad as it feels, and don't expect it ever to get better. They tell the larger society that disability and illness equal misery, so there's no need to bother about making our lives good. There's an easy way out."

Johnson acknowledges the possibility of individual situations where assisting a suicide or looking the other way might be morally right. "But I wouldn't try to objectively define those situations and build law around them," she says. "It just can't be done. Killing is too serious to manage by checklist."

And what of our physical vulnerability? "We are living the lives that others fear," says Johnson. "I depend on others to keep me alive every day. If I'm lucky, I get them to honor my requests—and keep me alive—on the strength of my paychecks and my charms. But money and charms are transient and, at bottom, we need people to know they're stuck with us no matter what and that they'll see us through those days when we feel bad about the pressures we put them under or when we get tired of all the complications."

With PAD, insurers may be less inclined to see us through. As a class, we're both poor and expensive; beer income, champagne needs. We're the medically unattractive. Of course we fear that insurers will deny us expensive treatment options while holding out the carrot of "a peaceful and dignified death." The cheapest care is no care. . . .

Choice and Control

"We are not a right-to-die group," wrote Drew Batavia, the president of AUTONOMY until his death in January. "We are a disability-rights organization that supports our right to decide issues of our lives. The unifying theme is choice and control."

Batavia and Hugh Gallagher co-founded AUTONOMY partly to fight Attorney General John Ashcroft's efforts to nullify Oregon's Death With Dignity Act, partly as a reaction to NDY. Batavia felt that while the leadership of many disability-rights groups opposes PAD and presumes to speak for all of us, many of the rank and file support it.

He may be right. In a 2001 Harris Poll, 68 percent of people with disabilities polled nationwide favored PAD. A small study by Pamela Faden shows a fairly even split, but she warns against using her survey to quantify consensus. Her study does show that many members of disability-rights groups fear criticism if they speak out in favor of PAD.

Batavia—but not necessarily AUTONOMY—saw personal autonomy as the primary goal, and solving social issues that surround PAD as secondary. This is not to say Batavia ignored such issues. To the contrary, his fingerprints are all over key legislation to remedy them. . . .

Gallagher, like NDY, objects to Hemlock's use of the word "hopeless" as a criterion for hastened death in much of its literature. "A sense of hopelessness is a call for help in living, not dying," he says. He emphasizes that AUTONOMY wants personal control during the dying process, not hastened death for people struggling with life.

Do the Oregon law's guidelines, as Johnson suggests, simply define a class considered better off dead? "Absolutely not," Gallagher says. "The Oregon law is reactive, not proactive. . . . It has the support of a large majority of its citizens. It's an insult to say Oregonians believe their terminally ill loved ones are better off dead. It cheapens and polarizes a serious moral issue."

Gallagher is not looking for conflict. "This is not a game of one team opposing another. Different people, cultures and religions hold different positions. These positions must be respected. AUTONOMY believes it should be up to the individual. Our whole purpose is to reduce the vulnerability of disabled persons to outside influence. We are grown-ups and we don't need Ashcroft telling us what we can or cannot do."

And Gallagher sets out his own credo: "I have fought hard to live my life as I choose to live it, to make my own life decisions. I will not give up this autonomy of decision making on my deathbed."

The Hemlock Society

Since Hemlock is headquartered in Denver, I know several of its principals. They are good, intelligent people who wonder why we demonize them and, equally, why we don't see that they promote choice, not coercion.

They don't want to kill people with disabilities. They don't want to kill anyone. They don't provide physical assistance in hastening death. They do provide counseling, information and support. They do support PAD legislation. They want all possible supports at the end of life, and oppose suicide for emotional or financial reasons. They say they address the agonies of dying, not the tribulations of living. . . .

A recent public-relations disaster occurred when Hemlock invited Philip Nitschke to address its national conference in San Diego. Nitschke, an Australian campaigner for euthanasia, advocates making "rational suicide" available to everyone from troubled teenagers to lonely old people. At the conference, he called [Dr. Jack] Kevorkian a hero and offended many Hemlock members by his immoderate zeal for suicide. Hemlock, for the record, has distanced itself from Kevorkian [who has been imprisoned for assisting suicides] and may now be edging away from Nitschke.

It hasn't helped that Nitschke receives funding from Hemlock to design machines people can use to kill themselves, or that he assisted in the very public death—21 family members and friends attended—of euthanasia advocate Nancy Crick, who reportedly was dying from a recurrence of bowel cancer. A postmortem found no sign of cancer, and Nitschke later admitted he was aware of Crick's cancer-free state.

But organizations can learn and change, and there are signs that Hemlock is doing just that. . . . Soon Hemlock will make another effort to alter its public image by changing its name. [In 2003 its name was changed to End-of-Life Choices, and in 2005 it united with Compassion in Dying and became Compassion & Choices.]. . .

PAD as Public Policy

Most unassisted suicides tend to be grotesque. They're violent or fail or create new disabilities. They exclude loved ones at a time when closure is needed. Wouldn't the option of PAD be better than that?

"I think it ought to remain difficult and messy," says Harriet Johnson, "something you'd think about pretty hard before doing. I don't see every suicide as irrational or even tragic. However, I have no trouble following NDY in toto when it comes to the law, which is what NDY is really about. Killing should remain a criminal act. When it's discovered, we should prosecute. But the law isn't the same as justice and never will be. It serves too many conflicting purposes to represent any kind of ideal."

So to serve justice, at times, we should ask someone to bend or break the law for us? That's hard on the someone else.

"As it ought to be. Gut-wrenching, bone-chilling agony." . . . Johnson thinks Oregon's restriction of its PAD law to people with six months to live is suspect. "It's really illogical to give them, and only them, the right to a quick and easy out. I agree with Kevorkian that if anyone 'needs' death services it's people with a long life expectancy who are miserable. I don't quite understand why the lines are drawn the way they are. But then, I reject the whole idea of line-drawing."

So we should offer PAD to everyone or no one?

"To no one." "I believe that whether or not to continue living is as personal a choice as anyone could make," says [psychologist] Lauri Yablick, "and that helping people die is potentially as valid a role for health-care providers as helping them live." But legalizing PAD? "No. Not here, not now, and given our health-care system, not for a long time. This is such a complicated issue and people want to treat it so simply."

Yablick questions the Oregon law's lack of consistency and inclusion. "The Oregon Act excludes most people with mental conditions. Who sold the myth that we can make a clear, reliable and objective determination of competency and emotional stability? Where's the logic in excluding people with depression and other serious mental illness—groups with the highest rates of suicide—from the sanctioned version? Won't people with progressive dementias still feel pressured to act prematurely? Who decided that physical suffering trumps emotional suffering?

"Another great fallacy is that regulations prevent abuses," she says. "[The] Ten Commandments didn't bring a loving and peaceful world. More laws didn't bring fewer prisons. And the regulations intended to prevent other health-care abuses have failed miserably. I know in every finger, toe and split end that widespread acceptance [of PAD] will result in further abuse." . . .

"The law has to be crafted for the most vulnerable members of society," Yablick reminds us. "The law is for everybody. How can we support hastened death under these circumstances? It's a choice I want available for me and for everyone I love, but it's just too damn costly."

Suicide Is a Personal Decision

The law is for everybody. Viewed through that framework, some of the pieces shift into place and some go skittering off the puzzle board. What you make of PAD is your business, but here's where I landed after I made it mine:

After all the discussion, suicide remains a personal matter. Individuals, not organizations, commit suicide. We shouldn't moralize or psychologize after the fact.

Suicide aided by laypeople who provide knowledge and support—Hemlock's sort of assistance—raises the ante. More people participate and coercion, by others or by circumstance, becomes a greater concern. Yet Hemlock and other programs like it provide an alternative to PAD, and perhaps a better one. They enable facing death peacefully in the home, after the goodbyes are said, with friends and family present.

If we really want the option of hastening death, and if Hemlock were to drop its advocacy for PAD and concentrate on what it already does—take the P out of PAD—I'd be tempted to say it's the best way we can provide some autonomy in end-of-life decisions without opening the door to systemic abuse.

True, utilizing Hemlock's help can send a terrible message about disability, but it's a gentler message than legalizing PAD. And what message do we send if we allow ourselves to linger through intractable pain, dementia, through it all, whatever we've got, into nothing? Won't people say, "I wouldn't want to die that way"? Is it so bad to end a good life with a good death?

PAD is an enormous escalation from suicide, either solitary or in the company of others. It makes our end-of-life choices the province of law, medicine and economics, as implemented by a deeply flawed health-care system. My fear is that PAD will become a constant presence in health-care settings, a big friendly mutt that lays its head in our laps and wags its lethal invitation whenever we doubt our ability to go on.

Physician-Assisted Suicide Is Compatible with Christian Ethics

John Shelby Spong

The Right Reverend John Shelby Spong is the retired bishop of the Episcopal diocese of Newark, New Jersey. He is the author of many books, including the best-sellers Rescuing the Bible from Fundamentalism *and* Why Christianity Must Change or Die. *In the following selection he explains why he believes physician-assisted suicide is an acceptable, and even desirable, option from the standpoint of Christian ethics. Bishop Spong declares that when a terminally ill person is in hopeless pain or has lost dignity through dependence on painkilling medication, it is a basic human right for that person to choose how and when to die, and that this right should be guaranteed by law. In his opinion, when medical science is simply postponing the reality of death, the sacredness of life is no longer being served.*

It is a unique experience for a representative of the Christian church to be invited to contribute to a book on the issue of choice at the end of human life. Typically, this is not an arena in which traditional Christians feel comfortable. Although the church has by and large made peace with what is generally called "passive euthanasia"—that is, the suspension of artificial life-support systems to allow death to take its natural course—organized religion generally draws the line at that boundary. For me, however, that limitation is a sign of an unwillingness to debate the real issues. This reticence is based on certain unspoken moral presuppositions that I believe have simply become inoperative through the remarkable advances in medical knowledge and technology. Far from being the place where the debate ends, in my mind "passive euthanasia" is where the real discussion begins.

Because I will be viewed by some religious leaders as a distinctively minority voice, I find it necessary to state my credentials by starting this chapter with a brief spiritual autobiography. . . . I identify myself first and foremost as a committed and practicing Christian. I have never lived apart from that identity. . . . I wanted to do nothing but be a priest from the time of my earliest memory. . . . I served my church as a priest for twenty-one years. My church elected me to be one of its bishops when I was forty-four years old. I served as a bishop for twenty-four years, retiring in 2000 as the senior sitting Episcopal bishop in the United States. Far from being a fringe voice, I am someone who has lived at the heart of the Christian church. I have no context from which to address these end-of-life issues other than that of one who has spent my personal and professional life deep inside the boundaries of organized religion.

Assisted Suicide Is a Moral Option for Christians

Yet I am passionate in my conviction that the time has come when Christians must relinquish their negativity toward those activities that are aimed at assistance in dying, active euthanasia, and physician-assisted suicide. I see all of these initiatives as being within the religious context, which begins with the assertion that life is holy and that this holiness must be served in all we do. It is from the standpoint of what I define as Christian ethics, which are rooted in the sacredness of life, that I bear my witness that assisted suicide can and does operate within that specifically religious framework.

I believe that if and when a person arrives at that point in human existence when death has become a kinder alternative than hopeless pain and when a chronic dependency on narcotics begins to require the loss of personal dignity, then the basic human right to choose how and when to die should be guaranteed by law and respected by our communities of faith. I have spoken publicly in favor of this conviction for years but always assumed that I was a lonely single voice within my church. Then I decided to test that premise; in my role as bishop, I appointed a task force in our diocese to study these issues and to bring their conclusions to our diocese's decision-making body for a vote up or down. . . .

After a year of study, including open hearings across the state, this task force drafted a report to place before the convention of the Diocese of Newark. . . . After a three-hour public debate, covered by all the major media from the metropolitan New York area, this convention endorsed, by a two-to-one majority, physician-assisted suicide "as a moral option for Christians." That convention was made up of 600 people, approximately 450 of them elected lay people and 150 ordained clergy from our various and diverse congregations. This was one of the first times that an official body within a mainline Christian church in the United States had taken a positive stand on this question. . . .

Christians Must Not Refuse Responsibilities

As a Christian, I affirm [the] conviction that life is sacred, that it is the ultimate gift from God. Because I hold this belief, I am committed to living every moment I am given as deeply, richly, and fully as I can. However, the times in which we live, as well as the shape of our developed consciousness in many areas of life, have changed dramatically through the ages. Christians must also take cognizance of that.

Human knowledge has expanded enormously, which means that "new occasions teach new duties," as the poet James Russell Lowell once observed. I today can no longer just quote the biblical wisdom of antiquity as if that is the final answer to anything. I cannot be just a passive observer of life.

It is not enough simply to assert that I am a committed Christian. I am also a citizen of the twenty-first century. I must take my place in history seriously.

I am the beneficiary of a vast revolution in scientific and medical thinking. I possess a reservoir of data that was not available to the people who wrote the Bible. This is the gift of the modern world to me. I have watched life expectancy expand remarkably. I live in a world of quadruple heart by-passes, radiation and chemotherapy, laproscopic surgical procedures, organ transplants, prostate specific antigen tests, Pap smears, miracle drugs, and incredible life-support systems. My grandfather died of pneumonia, before the development of penicillin. I have had two diseases that I do not believe my grandparents would have survived.

I live in a privileged part of the world and in a privileged generation. I rejoice in all of these human achievements. Let there be no mistake, however, about what is happening. These stirring achievements represent human beings' taking on the power we once ascribed only to God. We have, by our own knowledge and expertise, put our hands on the decisions regarding life and death. We cannot and must not now refuse to engage these decisions at the end of our own lives. We have pushed back the boundaries of death inexorably. We have enabled this generation to live in a way that previous generations could never have imagined. We have watched human life actually evolve to a point at which it must accept Godlike responsibilities. The time has come to celebrate that, not to hide from it in the language of piety.

I see the religious community today trembling in the face of our own human audacity and seeking to hide from the responsibility inherent in our own human achievements, none of which we would be willing to surrender. Why else would we hesitate before this final boundary called death? Why would we resist so vigorously the reality that now we must take a hand in our death decisions? When medical science expands the boundary and the quality of life, Christians do not complain. Rather, we rejoice because we believe it affirms our conviction that life is holy.

It is one thing, however, to expand life and quite another to postpone death. When medical science shifts from expanding the length and quality of life and begins simply to postpone the reality of death, why are we not capable of saying that the sacredness of life is no longer being served, and therefore Christians must learn to act responsibly in the final moments of life?

What happens to both our courage and our faith? Is a breathing cadaver, with no hope of restoration, an example of the sacredness of life? Is intense and unrelieved suffering somehow a virtue? I do not think so. Do we human beings, including those of us who claim to be Christians, not have the right to say, "That is not the way I choose to die?" I believe we do.

Death Is Not the Enemy of Humanity

Is death really the enemy of our humanity, as St. Paul once stated? Much Christian thinking has been based on that definition. Well, let it be said by a bishop of the church: *St. Paul was wrong*—here and in several other places. . . . Paul was a child of his era, responding to his own presuppositions and living with his own prejudices. They are not my presuppositions. I prefer to think of death not as an enemy but as a friend, even a brother, as St. Francis of Assisi once suggested. The time has therefore come, I believe, for Christians to embrace death not as an enemy to be defeated but as an aspect of life's holiness to be embraced.

Death is life's shadow. It walks with us through the course of our days. We embrace death as a friend because we honor life. I honor the God of life whom I serve by living fully. It does not honor God to cling to an existence that has become an empty shell.

I do not honor life when I fail to see that death and finitude are what give our humanity its precious quality. Death is not a punishment for sin, as Paul also once suggested and as classical Christianity has long maintained. Death is an aspect of life, a vital aspect that gives life its deepest flavor, its defining sensitivity.

Death has a way of ringing the bell on all procrastination. It is because life is finite, not infinite, that we do not postpone the quest for meaning indefinitely. It is because of the presence of death with us on our life's journey that we do not fail to take the opportunity to say "I love you," to invest ourselves in primary relationships, to do what needs to be done now, not tomorrow, to build a better world now. Death says you do not have forever to make a difference. Death is what gives conscious life its uniqueness. Remove death from life and life becomes enduring boredom, an endless game of shuffleboard. We make life precious by embracing the reality of death, not by repressing it or denying it. . . .

I, for one, want to live my life by squeezing every ounce of joy out of every moment I am given. I want to expand my life to its fullest extent. That is the way I choose to affirm the sacredness of life. I want to drink deeply of life's sweetness, to scale its heights and plumb its depths. I want to do all I can do to affirm life and, yes, to postpone death at least until life's quality has been so compromised that it is no longer life as I believe God intended it. At that time I want to embrace death as my friend, my companion who has walked with me from the moment of my birth.

I want to live my days surrounded by those I love, able to see my wife's beautiful smile and feel the touch of her hand. I want to share in the joy and vitality of my children and grandchildren. When those realities are taken away, I want to leave this world, and those I love, with a positive vision. I want them to see in me one who lived and loved deeply and well until living and loving deeply and well was no longer possible.

I want them to remember me as a person who was vital to the end, in possession of all that makes me who I am, and as one who died well. My deepest desire is always to choose death with dignity over a life that has become either hopelessly painful and dysfunctional or empty and devoid of all meaning.

That is the only way I know that would allow me to honor the God in whose image I was created. That is the way I want to acknowledge the relationship I have had with God, which has grown from a dependent and immature one into the maturity of recognizing that to be human is to share with God in the ultimate life-and-death decisions. That is how I hope and expect to celebrate life's holiness and to honor life's creator. That does not seem to me to be too much to ask my faith to give me or my government to guarantee for me.

Choosing Death with Dignity Should Be Legal

I think this choice should be legal. I will work, therefore, through the political processes to seek to create a world in which advance directives are obeyed and physicians assist those who so choose to die at the appropriate time. I also think the choice to do this should be acclaimed as both moral and ethical—a human right, if you will; and I will work through the ecclesiastical processes of my church and all the forces of organized religion to change consciousness, to embrace new realities, and to enable Christians and other people of faith to say that we are compelled in this direction because we believe that God is real and that life is holy. The God whom I experience as the source of life can surely not be served by those in whom death is simply postponed or not allowed to serve its natural function.

Physician-Assisted Suicide Is Not Compatible with Christian Ethics

Archbishop Peter Jensen

The Most Reverend Peter Jensen is archbishop of the Anglican Diocese of Sydney, Australia. He is a leading theologian and the former head of Moore Theological College. In the following selection Jensen discusses physician-assisted suicide from a Christian standpoint. Jensen argues that one great test of morality is love of others, but in his opinion allowing assisted suicide would not show love. Furthermore, if it were considered normal it might lead to viewing the elderly and incapacitated as burdensome. It may also prompt the disabled or infirm to choose death to avoid becoming a burden on their families. Finally, Archbishop Jensen asserts that humans should not play God in determining the fate of oneself for others. People, in Jensen's opinion, should "continue to work towards life."

The case in favour of voluntary euthanasia [i.e. physician-assisted suicide] is powerful, clear and simple. It consists of two parts. First there is the relief of suffering. When faced with the suffering, mental or physical, of the terminally ill, and when faced with the prospect or the actuality of our own suffering, we determine to prevent it. We do not allow fatally ill animals to suffer; why should we stand by and see humans go through pain which is beyond help and for no good purpose? The great virtue of compassion should move us to allow this for others even if we do not allow it for ourselves.

Secondly, there is the rights of the individual. Where a person is of a sufficient age to take responsibility, and where

Archbishop Peter Jensen, "Can Euthanasia Be Voluntary?" Address at Westmead Hospital, March 18, 2003. Reproduced by permission of the author.

the person's reason is sound, they must have the right to make their own choice about their life. Others must not make this choice for them. . . .

Assisted Suicide Is a Dangerous Idea

Despite these arguments I am going to say that the acceptance of voluntary euthanasia would be very dangerous indeed, and would change the nature of the health care professions. There are a number of problems with the proposal, but the difficulty I want to address today is this: I do not think that we can truly talk of euthanasia being voluntary. I realise that talk of individual rights has become very persuasive in the contemporary world. It seems to be fundamental to the way we think and view each other and ourselves. But it is worth noting that this is not the only possible way of viewing the world. There is really clash of philosophies here. The triumph of the individualistic philosophy is at the expense of what may be called 'relational philosophy'. Your choice about voluntary euthanasia may well depend upon whether you favour an individualistic or a relational philosophy.

Voluntary euthanasia is to be distinguished from that euthanasia made infamous by Nazism during the 1930s and 1940s in which mentally incapable and elderly patients were summarily executed, being regarded as dangerous to the genetic make-up of the people and as a burden to the State. . . . We all agree that whatever happens we must not have a society in which people are killed simply because they are old, incapable or decayed. The free, mature consent of the individual is crucial.

Furthermore, in speaking of voluntary euthanasia we are not directly addressing those agonising decisions about the end of life which so frequently face the medical profession. Since the whole ethos of the profession has always been toward the preservation of life, doctors have, if anything, erred on the side of keeping life going. Despite the consultation with relatives there remains a loneliness inevitably attendant upon the physician's choice to cease striving, to allow the patient to die. Indeed there are legitimate choices about palliative care which may as a side-effect, so to speak, shorten the dying process. Someone has to make these decisions; we feel that there ought to be rational and ethical grounds for making them; we rightly hope that the relatives or, if possible, the patient may relieve us of the moral burden of the decision. . . .

Thus, by introducing the word 'voluntary', the advocates of assisted suicide are making the necessary point that euthanasia can only be morally justified when it is agreed to by the subject, when a mature and balanced individual is making the decision for himself or herself. The word 'voluntary' suggests that we are taking personal responsibility, unaffected by internal factors that would distort the thinking process or external factors such as the manipulation of others. Consistent advocates of voluntary euthanasia recognise, therefore, that suicide is not just the province of the terminally ill. Such responsibility is able to be exercised by people of all ages (from adolescence onwards) and in all states of health. That is to say, a person may be able to commit themselves to voluntary euthanasia before they grow sick and even elderly. There is an important principle at stake here to which I will return.

Is Suicide an Individual Right?

Can we legislate for a euthanasia which will truly be voluntary? Let's start by thinking about suicide itself. Have we got a right to take our own lives? Suicides used to be condemned totally and victims even buried in unconsecrated ground. Today we have a far greater sympathy with those who take their lives, and recognise that such an act is easily done at a time of immense stress or even by people who are mentally ill. Nonetheless, in general terms no responsible person advocates suicide or sees the suicide rate as anything else than tragic. Do we really want to say that suicide is a right for the individual?

Most of us agree that one of the great tests of morality is of love for others. 'You must love your neighbour as yourself' is the rule of morality widely accepted, if not practised. In a contemporary world our emphasis on human freedom and our determination to act as independent agents means that we think of suicide as a purely individual action. In fact, however, there are few suicides which do not have a major impact on others. The death of a loved person is always sad and some-times tragic, but there is a special grief associated with suicide, a grief followed by feelings of guilt, despair and helplessness. In a profound sense, suicide reaches out and touches the lives of anyone who loves him or her. It is a declaration that I have nothing more to give you and you can receive nothing from me. We can come to understand the victim and our own rela-tionship with him if there is a question of mental illness. It is very hard to accept the verdict of an otherwise sane person who chooses to leave our relationships in this way, even under conditions of extreme illness. Does it show love?

Even more significantly, we must recognise the reality of the copy-cat effect. When a suicide occurs in a community such as a school or college, or even in the wider community, it stimulates others to do the same. My suicide may be all about me; but it makes it easier for others to do the same, and so fails the test of love.

There is another point. When we talk about voluntary eu-thanasia it is usually the case that we are thinking of assisted suicide. In order for the suicide to be successful and not botched, advice is given, and others have to enter into the ac-tual administration. If the advocates for voluntary euthanasia are aware of the possible abuses of euthanasia they will insist on elaborate legal precautions. These also involve a number of others in the whole activity. In short, my suicide is never a matter for myself alone, but is one in which the community as a whole, and individuals within it, have to take a similar re-sponsibility for me or are deeply affected by the choice I have made.

Making Assisted Suicide Legal Would Lead to Making It Normal

This will be particularly clear if the community ever introduces assisted suicide. By making it legal we will have taken a step towards making it normal. By providing the necessary help we, as a community, will have involved ourselves in the moral decision that suicide can be justifiable, depending only on the choice of the individual. Is that a good message to send? We are not mere individuals. We always need, and involve others, which brings us to the hub of the problem: the clash between the individualistic and the relational philosophies of life.

Can euthanasia be voluntary? . . . The problem, of course, is in establishing that a really sick person is sufficiently mature, balanced and independent for a decision of this nature. Terminally ill patients precisely may not meet this test. Certainly, as we all know, acute pain, physical or mental, diminishes our independence and distorts our view of the world. Can a person in such pain make a decision which can be called 'voluntary'? The example of torture suggests that the word 'voluntary' is the wrong category for such a situation. A person in acute pain may seek release through death where palliative care, properly administered, may change the mood entirely.

Terminally ill patients want a dignified death; that is not to say that they want a premature one. Advocates of voluntary euthanasia appeal to our sense of compassion. But compassion needs eyes to see what is compassionate in a given situation. Surely the way of love is to provide the best palliative care and to surround the elderly and especially the terminally ill with the best and most compassionate care that we can provide. My fear is that the advent of voluntary euthanasia will end with us seeing the elderly, the incapacitated and long-term patients as burdensome. Indeed, I am told that some of the early evidence from the Netherlands showed doctors taking decisions about life and death into their own hands. The very ethos created by voluntary euthanasia will make it hard to respect the alleged voluntary aspect of it.

But there is a more profound question still. To what extent do any of us make completely voluntary decisions in the sense needed for voluntary euthanasia to become moral? Despite the attempt of our society to say that we are, above all, individuals, the fact of the matter is that human beings are communal creatures and understand ourselves in the light of what others think about us.

Patients' Decisions Will Depend on What They Think Others Want

The question of whether a patient wants voluntary euthanasia would not, therefore, be settled by the patient making a mature and independent decision on their own. Such cases may perhaps occur, but they will become rarer as time goes on. It will be settled in case after case by what the patient thinks others around him or her to do.... There is a constant sense of helplessness for the patient within the hospital system. They depend upon [medical professionals]. Furthermore, it is a notorious fact that patients frequently misunderstand what doctors tell them. The fault may lie with the poor communication skills of the doctor. It may frequently lie with the stress and sense of helplessness of the patient. The most intelligent patients frequently misunderstand the reality of their situation. All the more is this the case when a disease is potentially or actually fatal. They will want to know whether [the doctor] thinks that it is time for them to exit: and [he] will not always know that they are reading the signals in [his] tone, in [his] manner. 'My' right to assisted suicide will impact unfavourably on your right to continue to live to the end.

The death of a patient, however elderly, has very significant consequences in family life. It is frequently a turning point. The burden of looking after an elderly relative is now finished; an estate, perhaps a very rich estate, will now be divided. The patient is looking for advice and help about what they should do from the very people who will be most deeply affected by their death. In many cases, that death will be received with relief or even gratitude. Can we ever be sure that even the most loving family will not by covert or overt means point the patient towards an assisted suicide which will not be their true desire or even be in their best interests?

But there is something even more sinister here. At present our society as a whole, and hence our medical profession, believe in keeping alive. However, with the advent of the baby boomers into the latter end of their lives, the health services are going to be faced with a massive overload with vast financial implications. So far, our governments have resisted calls for voluntary euthanasia. Who can say, faced with the gigantic financial burden yet to be shouldered by the community, that governments will not accede to voluntary euthanasia primarily for fiscal reasons? In that event, the medical profession, so long regarded as a life giving force in the community, will also become the deliverers of death. The patient will never be able to be sure whether the advice given by his or her medical professional is activated by the interests of the patient or the needs of the system. I believe . . . health professionals with the highest standards, . . . will already have seen the possibilities of this in a system which is groaning even now. [They] will, I am sure, have resisted it, but it is difficult to resist the whole system if it is based covertly on a new and ambiguous principle.

I conclude with comments based on two experiences. The first, was observing at close range over a number of years, the death from cancer of my own mother. I knew of her indomitable will to live even to the end despite the suffering. I knew also that if one of us as members of her family had ever said to her that we would like her to go, in order that we did not suffer from her sufferings, she would have volunteered to exit earlier. Indeed we would not have had to say anything; a hint from us plus a system in which assisted suicide was a possibility, and she would have demanded her own death, hiding her true feelings from us. Her so-called voluntary euthanasia would have arisen from the manipulation of her family.

Christianity's Chief Value Is Love, Not Freedom

The second experience is that of being a Christian. The Bible clearly endorses the relational rather than the individualistic idea of being human. The view of the Bible is far more realistic than that of the modern individualistic philosophy with all its talk about 'my rights'. The Bible does not see us merely as individuals. In the biblical word the individual is cherished. He or she is in the image of God, of that there is no doubt. On the other hand, the Bible sees us as parts of communities. The Bible's chief value is not freedom but love. In fact, it sees love as the basis of true freedom. More than that, the Bible also teaches us, and everyday experience confirms it, that human beings cherished and loved as they are by God, are deeply flawed. There is evil in our hearts as well as good. We cannot be trusted to be consistently and entirely good. We cannot trust ourselves and we cannot trust others.

The claim for voluntary euthanasia depends upon the philosophy that we are primarily individuals and it depends upon our view of human nature in which good will triumphs. The truth of the matter is that, despite our compassion for the suffering and the urge we may have to help another person end their suffering rather than endure it, we cannot afford to take this responsibility upon ourselves. Even if in an individual case our motives are entirely good, the individual case must not open the doors for a general practice in which so often motives will be mixed or even worse. Our danger is that we are attempting to do a god-like thing without the power, wisdom or goodness of God.

What can we do? We should resist the call for voluntary euthanasia. We should continue to work towards life. We must continue to allow the dying to die, and we must do all we can to comfort their passing, to use our resources to relieve their pain, and to use our human resources to keep them in loving relationship until they pass from our help entirely. This, I think, is the path of wisdom; I am sure that it is the path that compassion needs to tread.

CHAPTER 4

Personal Narratives On Assisted Death

A Disabled Woman Tells Why She Opposes Withdrawal of Medical Life Support

Diane Coleman

Diane Coleman is an attorney and the executive director of the Progress Center for Independent Living in Forest Park, Illinois, a nonprofit organization advocating on behalf of people with disabilities. She is also the founder and president of Not Dead Yet, a national grassroots disability rights organization opposing the legalization of assisted suicide and euthanasia. In the following selection, Coleman describes how she felt seeing the 2004 movie Million Dollar Baby, *in which a disabled woman prefers to die rather than live on a ventilator. Coleman finds the movie disturbing because it fosters the idea that disabled people would be better off dead and that it is admirable of them to choose death instead of living with a disability. Coleman argues that the movie's resolution is a reflection of society's prejudice against the disabled and of a pernicious belief that a disabled life is not worth living.*

Many people have told me that they don't think they could "stand to live" if they needed a wheelchair like me. That's why I felt a little queasy about going to see *Million Dollar Baby*. But helping plan the first disability protest of the movie, in Chicago, I had a duty to see it.

I thought I was emotionally well-prepared. I already knew many details about the last half hour—the injury, hospital, nursing home and killing scenes—from disabled colleagues.

But my preparation was more than that. When I grew up, through braces and surgeries, my elementary school teachers

Diane Coleman, "Seeing Million Dollar Baby from My Wheelchair," *Not Dead Yet*, February 2005. Reproduced by permission.

called me "Mary Sunshine." When I completed UCLA law school from a motorized wheelchair, I was called "inspirational." I took it as the highest compliment to be told by some non-disabled person that they "didn't think of" me as "handicapped." When I was excluded or rejected in my work or social life, I could always understand the other's perspective.

Even the few times someone would actually say they would rather be dead than be like me, I would just politely forge on.

In my early thirties, sharing experiences with disabled friends, I finally learned how to recognize and constructively resist discrimination. The connection and insights we shared gave me a new lens through which to view my life. Most importantly, I learned to look more clearly at the ways I had internalized the stigma and shame of disability, and began the lifelong struggle to undo the damage done by growing up in isolation from a true sense of community and mutual respect.

In short, a "Jerry's Kid" became a "telethon protester." Over the last two decades of involvement in the disability rights movement, I have faced arrest many times in non-violent protest to help win the right to ride the bus, and the right to not be forced into a nursing home because of the need for assistance to live. During [Dr. Jack] Kevorkian's heyday in assisting the suicides of middle-aged disabled women, I founded a national disability rights group called Not Dead Yet. Using a ventilator at night since 2002, it's become even more personal.

Seeing *Million Dollar Baby* from My Wheelchair

I came into the theater, wanting to flee quickly when *Million Dollar Baby* was over. I sat through the whole movie without removing my coat, scarf, hat or gloves.

Queasy stomach, wish to flee—not typical for me anymore. Moreover, the threat of assisted suicide and euthanasia are daily fare for Not Dead Yet. We fight to be heard over the loud voices of players on both sides whose interests should be readily seen as, at best, secondary to the organized voice of those society says are "better off dead." So many of us have died too young, never getting a real chance to live.

In the midst of all that reality, what makes a fictional movie like *Million Dollar Baby* so disturbing that I want to flee?

As the movie unfolded to its star-powered conclusion, audience members sniffled in pitiful admiration of Maggie's determination to die rather than move on and leave her non-disabled life behind. They were deeply moved by Frankie's redemption through fatherly love, his wish to help her live and his profound sacrifice in giving up everything he had to free her from her "frozen" body. This is the bittersweet ending that inspires so much acclaim.

As I watched, I thought about the impact the movie would have on severely disabled people surrounded only by doctors, nurses and mixed up, grieving family and friends.

Swept along in the emotion, could any audience member imagine a happy and meaningful life for Maggie as a quad? For him or herself as a quad?

Disability Is Not Worse Than Death

It took me another week to get in touch with my deeper personal discomfort.

Could people imagine a happy and meaningful life for me? Could they see that I am not living a fate worse than death?

I've always felt a tension between how others see me and how I see myself. By now, that tension, and my coping mechanisms, are way below the surface. Denial, the fantasy of acceptance, I have used whatever I could to endure and manage over 50 years of those looks, and looks away, to be who I am out in the world everyday.

But now I am forced to see how critics and audiences love this movie, resent our anger, and extol the virtues of open public discussion of euthanasia based on disability. My fantasy is ripped away.

If I'd been truly prepared, I'd have brought a sign to hold up, saying, "I Am Not Better Off Dead." I would have looked into every face exiting the theater, insisting that they see me, and this simple yet apparently incomprehensible message.

A Former Governor of Oregon Tells Why She Favors the State's Physician-Assisted Suicide Law

Barbara Roberts

Barbara Roberts was governor of Oregon from 1991 to 1995. The following selection is her foreword to the book Compassion in Dying: Stories of Dignity and Choice, *which contains the personal stories of terminally-ill Oregonians who chose to end their lives by physician-assisted suicide. In it she describes how Oregon's physician-assisted law was passed and why she favors it. Roberts's husband, a state senator, was a strong supporter of the right of individuals to have options in end-of-life matters. Later, he died a prolonged death from cancer before Oregon's Death with Dignity Act reached the ballot. Roberts says that he would be proud to know that his progressive legislation moved forward and that patients in a situation similar to his now have a choice. She believes that Oregon has become a role model for death with dignity.*

Life is a terminal condition. Death will come to each of us. Yet, if there is anything Americans wish to avoid discussing, find more threatening to face, and routinely skip making preparations for, it is our own inevitable death.

I have come to understand that dying is more difficult in a culture of denial. Grieving is more painful and lonely in a society of silence.

As a native Oregonian and a former governor, I am frequently asked by nonresidents how Oregon's Death with Dignity Law ever came to pass. Let me answer with a short history lesson on Oregon's aid in dying law.

The law came to the Oregon ballot as a citizen sponsored initiative in November 1994. The measure passed on a squeaker vote—winning by a 51 percent margin. A court challenge by the National Right to Life Committee kept the law from going into effect. That lawsuit's failure put the law back in the legislature's hands. The 1997 legislative session spent months arguing over the details of implementation, looking for improved legal and medical safeguards, and continually implying that Oregon voters did not know what they were doing when they passed that landmark law. So, in its political wisdom, unable to find improvements, the 1997 legislature placed a repeal of the original Act on the November ballot. This time the voters made their message very clear—the voters approved the law with a 60 percent margin.

After two well-funded, controversial statewide campaigns, Oregon voters became the best informed Americans on the subjects of dying, pain medication, heroic medical procedures, advance directives, and hospice care. Every television-viewing evening brought our citizens the pro and con positions on the ballot measure. Ad after ad detailed opinions on dying. Strong opinions filled letters-to-the-editor sections, editorial columns, front pages, and radio airwaves. Family and friends discussed the proposal over dinner, at bowling alleys, at hair salons, in classrooms, and churches and synagogues. Dying was out of the closet in Oregon.

What Led to Oregon's Law

But there is another important piece of the story—an earlier history. Dating back to the 1980s, a small number of Oregonians were asking questions about the dying process. Why should pain medications be withheld or limited for dying patients? Did advance directives and living wills have the force of law? As medical science advanced and the means to keep patients alive with machines grew more common, when did patients and families have the right to say, "Enough"? Many senior citizens expressed a greater fear of nursing homes and hospitals than actually dying. One of the most pressing questions became, "Doesn't how we die matter as much as how we live?"

My late husband, State Senator Frank Roberts, was one of those raising the questions. During his long legislative career he championed the rights of individuals to have options on end-of-life matters. He sponsored many bills, a number of which passed, that gave Oregonians, for example, the right to appoint a person to make health care decisions for them if they were unable to do so themselves. One bill assured a person's right to stop receiving extraordinary measures to keep him or her alive, including life support systems. On several occasions, Frank sponsored laws to allow terminal patients to hasten their death under carefully controlled conditions. In the political climate of the legislative process, those more controversial laws never left committee.

So why did Frank introduce all this legislation? He did so because he passionately and compassionately believed adults had the knowledge, ability, wisdom—and the right—to decide their own fate. And perhaps, looking back, he may have had some premonition of what was to come for him at the end of his own life. Frank died a prolonged and difficult cancer death. In the last weeks of his life he spoke often and wistfully of his proposed aid in dying legislation. But he did not live to see the Oregon measure reach the ballot or to celebrate the passage of Oregon's Death with Dignity Act in 1994.

In the final months of Frank's life, when I was Governor of Oregon and he was still serving as a State Senator, we spoke openly and publicly about his impending death. I believe our openness encouraged greater public discussion among all Oregonians about death and dying. I know for certain, if Frank were alive today, he would be proud to know his progressive legislation moved forward due to the efforts of this state's citizens and the initiative process. He would be comforted knowing the law has been rarely used and has worked without negative complications for the dying. He would applaud the work of Compassion in Dying. And he would not be surprised to find that many qualified terminal patients with the prescription in their refrigerator chose not to use it. Frank would fully understand the Oregonians who simply want the option and find comfort that the choice is available to them.

When Frank died at home in the Governor's residence on October 31, 1993, he had faced a terminal diagnosis for a year. He had been under hospice care for six months. In the last weeks of his illness he became the "poster child" for his right-to-die legislation. He was bed-ridden, suffered a stroke, was no longer able to eat, needed constant pain medication, and expressed his readiness to die. I did not want Frank to die—he was my love, my confidant, my friend. But, at that point, I couldn't wish for him to live any longer. Now, Oregon patients in a similar situation have a choice available to them. That was all Frank ever wanted for himself and others—choice.

Support for the Law Is Growing

In Oregon, even those who voted against the Death with Dignity Act and those who may still oppose it, can recognize clearly that Oregon has used the law sparingly with total adherence to the letter and the spirit of the Act. Plus, the word "dignity" has been the hallmark of this groundbreaking law. Oregon's law was carefully drafted with the safeguards and guidelines in the legal language that assured our citizens that such precautions would prevent abuse and misuse. Without those legal protections, Oregon voters never would have passed the measure.

I believe if the aid in dying law were on the ballot in Oregon in 2003, it would pass by 70 percent or more. And one of the strongest reasons for that growing support is the Compassion in Dying organization. Compassion has become the steward of our unique law. Since the law's implementation in 1997, Compassion has been the leading advocate and support organization for patients, families, physicians, and the law. Those who predicted a Kevorkian-like sideshow in Oregon have been silenced, one by one, as the law has been applied with care and compassion.

In the ten years since Frank's difficult death, I have learned much about the dying process in Oregon and America. I served on both the Oregon Hospice Association board of directors and the National Hospice Advisory Board. I am currently on the Advisory Board for Oregon Compassion in Dying. I spent part of a year as a volunteer in an AIDS hospice. Since the publication of my first book, *Death Without Denial, Grief Without Apology*, I have heard many personal stories of death and grief from individuals across the nation. I believe that which we can talk about we can make better.

I know this about Oregon: We lead the nation in the number of terminally ill patients enrolled in hospice. Oregon is one of the leaders in the use of morphine to treat pain for dying patients. We have more people die at home and fewer citizens die in intensive care units than anywhere in the nation. We are considered a model state in end-of-life care. Oregon's Death with Dignity Act has made the dying process an open and acceptable topic in Oregon communities and families. As we have ended the silence, progress has followed.

I am grateful to Oregon citizens for their vision and courage and compassion in caring so deeply about their fellow citizens. I hold those at Compassion in Dying in high regard for their ongoing dedication and their ability to face, first-hand, the terminally ill and to hold the hands and the hearts of those facing death.

A law is only as good as those who implement that law, and this nation should feel grateful to Oregon's voters and to Compassion in Dying for demonstrating the courage and wisdom to know when to acknowledge gently, "Enough."

Oregon has become the role model for death with dignity. We have drafted the blueprint for others to follow. In a culture of medical miracles and scientific expansion, we must not lose sight of the need to accept death as a realistic part of the life cycle.

An Oregon Doctor Tells Why He Opposes the State's Physician-Assisted Suicide Law

William M. Petty

William M. Petty is an Oregon physician and an associate professor of gynecology at the Oregon Health and Science University. The following selection is his testimony before the Hawaii House of Representatives, in which he tells why he opposes Oregon's physician-assisted suicide law and does not think other states should pass similar laws. Dr. Petty says that opponents of assisted suicide are right when they warn that legalization will adversely affect the most vulnerable people. He remembers patients who were manipulated by families or doctors into choosing suicide. He also states that prescriptions for lethal drugs are being given to patients whose judgment is impaired by depression. In addition, Dr. Petty points out that neither assisted suicides that fail nor abuses of Oregon's law are being reported, and, therefore, claims that the law works successfully are false.

I have spent my entire medical career in Oregon, treating patients with life threatening, sometimes terminal cancer. The issues raised by this legislation are ones I have dealt with my entire professional life. But I don't speak to you today about issues. I speak today about patients and their lives and the effect of physician-assisted suicide in my state.

Opponents of assisted suicide will warn you that it will affect the most vulnerable. They are right. For me the vulnerable have faces. They are patients I remember. I remember the woman talked out of pursuing further cancer treatment by her son. I remember the elderly woman: agitated, disoriented, and incoherent after her operation. The attending medical

William M. Petty, "Testimony before Hawaii House of Representatives," www.pccef .org, February 5, 2005. Reproduced by permission.

personnel repeatedly suggested to her daughter that the elderly woman be "let go," that she would not recover. I'm grateful that my wife refused this advice and that my "terminal" mother-in-law is leading a content life 11 months later.

Not all the vulnerable are so lucky. Some people are dependent on caregivers. They often focus on pleasing the caregiver. They are not in a position of independence and real choice. They are the potential victims of subtle or not so subtle coercion. Manipulation of patients is a real problem when physician-assisted suicide becomes an option. And this manipulation can't be prevented by writing legislative statutes, no matter how well intended. Manipulation can be done by a family member or the doctor.

Depression Impairs Judgment

I have counseled the suicidal, people who feel that today is intolerable, and tomorrow will be worse. A diagnosis of cancer is a very difficult thing to deal with. Depression is a reaction that can accompany that diagnosis. Depression does impair judgment. And that patient is vulnerable and not herself. This is not the time to abandon the person to physician-assisted suicide. Yet, in my state, doctors are giving suicide drugs to depressed patients. And there is nothing that requires that a patient be treated for depression before getting a lethal prescription. Psychiatric referrals have fallen each year the law has been in effect in Oregon until they are approaching zero.

This troubles me about my profession. In Oregon, it seems that physician attitudes are changing. Doctors are not trying to keep patients alive during the critical times. A friend with bladder cancer, which had spread, went to an oncologist and was told there was nothing more to do. Yet a second doctor said, "You have about an 80% chance of responding to treatment." My friend later asked about the first oncologist, "Do you think he is a 'death doctor'?" That was a question that wouldn't have been asked in my first 25 years of practice.

What is involved for the patient in assisted suicide? What happens? The patient needs to rapidly take 90 capsules worth of a barbituric acid, like Nembutal / pentobarbital. It takes this much to be lethal. It is extremely bitter. I've tasted it. It often causes severe abdominal pain and may cause nausea, vomiting and other problems.

Assisted Suicide Sometimes Fails

Does physician-assisted suicide fail? Yes it does. It fails about 20% of the time. In the book, "Drug Use in assisted Suicide and Euthanasia," discussing what has happened in the Netherlands, Dutch physician Gerrit Kimsma reports, "in 20% of the patients who received a barbiturate, a muscle relaxant was needed to end his life after the 5-hour period." What this means is that a lethal injection was given because the barbiturate didn't work. But in the years that physician-assisted suicide has been legal in Oregon, a suicide failure has never been officially reported.

There is a case from Oregon where a Portland man ingested the prescription at home with his wife and other family members present. He began having physical symptoms. It was not stated whether he was having abdominal pain, nausea & vomiting or what. His wife was greatly distressed and called 9-1-1. The man was taken to a local hospital and revived. He had completed all the paperwork the Oregon law required and was using a registered prescription. Yet this failure appeared in no report by the Oregon Department of Health. It became public only because it was discussed by an attorney at a meeting at Portland Community College. Pro-suicide activists, including the attorney, have publicly denied this case happened. But there was a tape recording of the meeting and I have a copy of it here. Does Hawaii want 911 calls for botched suicides?

Why is this important? Because it is a physician-assisted suicide failure in Oregon. This failure should have been reported. But it wasn't. There are other things not reported by authorities in Oregon, abuses or violations of the law that are now independently documented. The *Washington Post* reported Dr. Peter Rasmussen had a patient who took the suicide drugs. When he came back 11 hours later she was still alive. Why is this significant? Because the medications either cause death within 3 1/2–4 hours or the effect of the drug wears off. That is why doctors in the Netherlands give a lethal injection at five hours. The newspaper reports "the patient later died." How? No one is saying. Yet no one at Oregon's Department of Health has investigated. The law in Oregon doesn't provide for investigation. Nor does the law proposed in Hawaii.

There are more instances of abuse of the law in Oregon. So to say the law is successful is a fairytale. If no problems, abuses, or violations are ever reported, even if they occur, this doesn't mean the law is a success. It just means that the reports are unreliable.

The Law Harms Patients and Physicians

The law is not successful for vulnerable patients. The law is not successful for the medical profession because it has compromised the care provided by some physicians and protected other physicians who probably should have been investigated.

Let me close by telling you about two of my patients who did want suicide. I have had a plaque on the wall of my office, a part of the Hippocratic Oath, that says "I will give no poison nor recommend the same, but will hold all life to have inherent value." I have had many patients comment favorably on it, but two women objected to it.

The first woman had recurrent cancer and said she wanted to die. I asked her why. It turned out she had been stoically living with persistent pain. She wasn't completely responsive to her medication. When her pain medication was adjusted, her pain came under control. And she no longer wanted to die. She did die later, a natural death, and without pain. Modern medicine can control pain. We need to educate ourselves as physicians to be able to do this and for our patients to expect that this be done.

The second woman said she didn't like my plaque. I asked her why. It turned out she thought that if I were against physician-assisted suicide I would insist on keeping her on a respirator or artificial life support. I assured her that I would not do that. I would keep her comfortable, but her choice of treatments was her own. After this discussion, she understood that I would honor her wishes and she would control the course of her care. She later died a natural death at home.

My professional life has been involved in treating individual patients. The basis of our medical profession has been the innate value of each individual life. In Oregon we have now degraded medical care for thousands of individuals because 30 to 40 individuals annually legally kill themselves. We have certain doctors repeatedly involved in these suicides. The incomplete reports from Oregon falsely indicate that the law is a success.

I thank the Chair, Vice-Chair and members of the committee for allowing me this time to testify. I came from Oregon to give this testimony because physician-assisted suicide has harmed patients, my profession, and my state. It would not benefit the people of Hawaii either. I urge you to reject this legislation for the people of Hawaii.

A Reporter Witnesses a Legal Physician-Assisted Suicide in Oregon

Tim Christie

Tim Christie is a reporter for the Register-Guard, *the newspaper of Eugene, Oregon. The following selection is his account of the legal assisted suicide of Lucile Adamson. Adamson was 78 years old and was terminally ill with breast cancer. She had no family to care for her and lived alone, receiving services from a hospice. Once Adamson's cancer had spread through her body, she feared that she would soon be so incapacitated that she would have to rely on others for help in daily living. Although not in pain, she chose suicide because she did not want to become dependent. In the weeks before her death she took all the steps required under the law and a physician gave her a prescription for a lethal dose of medication. At the scheduled time two volunteers from the support group Compassion in Dying, one of whom was a retired doctor, went to her home. Along with Christie, whom Adamson allowed to be present, they witnessed her death.*

The white electric clock perched atop the television ticks away the last minutes of Lucile Adamson's life, marking the time until she is ready to drink six ounces of a bitter clear liquid that will stop her heart.

Adamson, 78, has been fighting breast cancer for 10 years and now the cancer has won. It has spread throughout her body, and doctors have stopped treatment. She finds just getting around her sparsely furnished apartment to be a painful struggle.

Adamson, a retired biochemist, moved to Eugene five years ago from Los Osos, Calif., attracted by the climate, nearby hiking trails and the college town atmosphere. Oregon's one-of-a-kind assisted suicide law was in the back of her mind as well, as she knew that someday she might have cause to put the law to use.

Now that day has come.

Wednesday, at about 12:30 p.m., Adamson committed suicide with a lethal dose of barbiturates prescribed by a doctor, joining the ranks of about 225 Oregonians who have done so [as of 2005] since the Death with Dignity Act took effect in 1998.

Adamson, who never married and has no children, was joined on her final day by two volunteers from Compassion in Dying of Oregon, a Portland-based group that helps dying patients navigate the law. Adamson also agreed to allow a reporter from the *Register-Guard* to be a witness to her death.

In an interview a week earlier, and in the last hour before she died, Adamson talked about her life, and about why she chose to end it on her own terms.

Fates Worse than Death

After her diagnosis, Adamson said she was able to live a mostly satisfactory life for about nine years, but her health "suddenly started going downhill" as the cancer spread about a year ago. Physician-assisted suicide, she said, "seemed the sensible thing to do."

With no appetite, she had lost 50 pounds in the last year. She could not stand up long enough to brush her teeth. She wore an eyepatch over her right eye, after radiation on a tumor behind her eye took her sight. She spent most of her time in bed or in a blue reclining chair in the corner of her living room.

"I saw no reason to continue since everything has become very difficult, from standing up to sitting down and everything in between," she said, "and with no prospects for improvement, but lots of prospects for much worse conditions than sudden death."

She said she feared suffering a stroke, or otherwise becoming incapacitated, and having to rely on others for daily living. "If you can have some choice about the matter, why not take it?" she said. "Get your affairs in order, and say goodbye, and not become dependent on someone else, which is important to me. I don't want to ask for help."

Adamson said she's not a religious person, and does not expect an afterlife. She also said she doesn't think the federal government has any business interfering in Oregon's law or deciding whether someone chooses to end her life.

A Full Life

Adamson grew up on a farm in Kansas, with no electricity and no running water, the second youngest of four siblings. The nearest church was seven miles down a muddy road, and the family did not have a religious upbringing, said her older sister, Gail Sims of San Luis Obispo, Calif. "Most of us are hard-headed realists," Sims said.

Adamson attended a one-room country grade school and graduated from Labette County Community High School in Altamont, Kan., in 1944. She had no desire to stay on the farm. "It was hard work, hot work," she said.

She went off to college instead, earning a bachelor's degree from Kansas State University and a master's at Iowa, and then a Ph.D. from the University of California at Berkeley in biochemistry.

It was during her time as a graduate student that James Watson and Francis Crick published their paper unlocking the secret of DNA, the elemental building block of life. And she spent much of her career exploring the mysteries of how chemical and biological processes work together in the body.

She was in charge of the medical lab at a Harvard hospital, and worked as a researcher and professor at the University of Hawaii and the University of Missouri. She also taught in Australia for a time on an exchange program. Later, she switched her focus to environmental health and helped start an ecology department at Howard University.

Her sister said she's not sure why Adamson never married, but she has an idea. "I suspect she was too smart for men in our age group to tolerate," Sims said. "She was smarter than the rest of us."

Adamson said she never got lonely. "I was never very social," she said. "I'm used to being alone."

Said her sister: "When you grow up on the plains of Kansas on your own farm, there's not much opportunity to develop a social attitude because there's no other people around."

When Adamson was well, she liked to hike and play bridge. When her body began to fail, books became her main companion.

On her bookshelf are a microscope, an atlas and books that indicate her broad interests: *Physics*, by Giancoli, and *Harrison's Principles of Internal Medicine*. William Sullivan's *100 Hikes in the Central Oregon Cascades*, and Audubon Society field guides to mushrooms and wildflowers. *Stupid White Men* by Michael Moore. A Charles Goren book on bridge. A worn black Bible, its spine peeling away. *The Worst Case Scenario Survival Handbook*. And poetry: *The Collected Poems of Robert Frost* and *The Oxford Book of American Verse* and multiple volumes of [poet] Ogden Nash.

Planning to Die

Adamson made her initial contact with Compassion in Dying of Oregon in January 2003. In July, as her health worsened, she got back in touch with the group so that she could take the final steps spelled out in Oregon law to legally commit suicide. By this time, she also was getting hospice services from Cascade Hospice in Eugene.

She made two oral requests for a lethal prescription from her doctor, 15 days apart. She provided a written request to her doctor, signed in the presence of two witnesses. Her doctor and a consulting physician confirmed her diagnosis and her prognosis—that she had less than six months to live—and determined that she was capable of making such a decision. And her doctor informed her of alternatives to suicide, including comfort care, hospice care and pain control.

Finally, her doctor prescribed her 10 grams of liquid Nembutal, the brand name for a barbiturate called pentobarbitol. On Friday, Aug. 5, a friend picked up the medication for her.

The following Monday Adamson makes final arrangements with Compassion in Dying: Two volunteers are scheduled to come to her apartment off Green Acres Road at 11:30 a.m. Wednesday.

At the appointed time, Dr. Nancy Krumpacker, a retired oncologist from Portland, and another volunteer, who declines to be identified, arrive at Adamson's apartment, and find her sitting in her easy chair in the corner of the living room, her feet propped up on a dining room chair. In keeping with Compassion in Dying's protocol, Krumpacker asks Adamson: Are you sure you want to do this?

Without hesitation or elaboration, Adamson responds emphatically: Yes.

At 11:28 a.m., Adamson takes some anti-nausea medicine—one tablet of Zofran and two tablets of Reglan—to ensure that she can keep the barbituates down, and then waits for the stipulated one hour before she can take her lethal dose of medicine.

On the floor next to her chair is the morning paper; a well-worn 1932 edition of *The Complete Short Stories of Somerset Maugham, Vol. 1*; and a denim Winnie the Pooh ball cap.

In the kitchen, Krumpacker, a trim woman with close-cropped gray hair and glasses, uses a pair of needle-nose pliers to peel the metal tops off four 2.5 gram bottles of Nembutal. When she is done, she pours the six ounces of liquid into a tall drinking glass, filling it not quite half full.

Adamson, wearing a striped shirt, blue slacks and slippers, says she is doing fine, and isn't nervous about dying—just ready.

"It's the thing to do," she says. "I feel I'm escaping all sorts of worse fates."

The Final Minutes

The room is momentarily quiet, the ticking clock the only sound, the shades drawn against a bright August day. Adamson breaks the silence by asking, "Should we play bridge until it's time for the end?" eliciting nervous laughter.

Krumpacker asks, "What do you think is going to happen after you swallow the medicine?"

Adamson, the scientist, responds, "I'll go to sleep. . . . You're not asking me about the afterlife, are you?"

"I'm just curious about what you think," Krumpacker says.

"Nothing," Adamson replies.

Krumpacker asks her about her research into environmental health, and they talk about the state of environmental degradation in the world until finally Adamson says, "I don't know if I want to spend my last minutes talking about this."

So instead she talks fondly about the cats she used to have, including Grey Ghost, a 14-pound gray male, and Theta and Mew, who would come into her room in the morning and meow loudly moments before Adamson's alarm would sound.

At 12:25 p.m., Adamson says, "Almost there—three minutes."

At 12:27 p.m., one minute shy of an hour, she says, "Why not do it?"

Krumpacker hands her the glass of Nembutal, and warns her that it's a bitter drink. "You might go to sleep very quickly; you want to drink it quickly, but not in big gulps."

At 12:28 p.m., Adamson takes her first swallow. "It's bitter," she says.

She takes a second draft, and a third. Krumpacker and the other volunteer kneel on either side of her chair. She keeps drinking—four, five, six, seven swallows, pausing between each—then coughs three times. Then she drinks down the rest, and hands the glass to Krumpacker. It all takes about a minute.

"A little bit went down the wrong way," she says, coughing again, then taking a swig of water from a bottle.

A moment passes, and Adamson says: "The bird is on the wing." She explains that it's a line from Omar Khayyam's *Rubaiyat*:

"The Bird of Time has but a little way

To Fly—and Lo! the Bird is on the Wing."

Adamson coughs again and rests her head in her right hand. Her eyes are closed now. Krumpacker watches her intently.

Death Comes Quickly

At 12:32 p.m. Krumpacker asks, "Are you still with us?"

"Yes," she responds, without opening her eyes.

At 12:34 p.m. her hand drops, and her head tilts back.

"Lucile?" Krumpacker says.

There is no response; Nancy looks at the other volunteer, and they nod. Adamson has fallen into a deep sleep, a coma, and she won't be waking up. The barbiturate is shutting down her respiratory system and her brain function, and slowing her heart muscle. Her head lolls to the right, and her mouth is slightly agape.

Krumpacker keeps close watch on Adamson now, and listens to her shallow breathing.

At 12:53 p.m., about 25 minutes after Adamson drank the Nembutal, Krumpacker places a stethoscope on her chest and listens for a heart beat. She hears none.

"She's gone," Krumpacker says.

She pats Adamson's arm and leg, and buttons her shirt. She calls Cascade Hospice and says, "This is Dr. Krumpacker here with Lucile Adamson, and she's just died."

Hospice officials will call the funeral home, and the funeral home will come to get Adamson and arrange for her to be cremated.

Krumpacker calls Adamson's attorney, and asks him to call Sims in California with the news.

Later, Krumpacker talks with Adamson's attending physician, filling him in on the details of the suicide, so that he in turn can report the case to the state Department of Human Services, which compiles the information into an annual report.

Later this month, Sims says, her son, the executor of Adamson's estate, will collect his aunt's remains.

"I suspect that he'll go out on some Oregon trails where we have all hiked and scatter her ashes." Sims says. "What she liked was hiking in the woods."

The Daughter of a Multiple Sclerosis Patient Ponders the Morality of Assisted Suicide

Yvette Cabrera-Rojas

Yvette Cabrera-Rojas was an undergraduate student at the University of Louisville, Kentucky, at the time the following essay was written. It won second place among over 500 entries in the contest for the 2002 Elie Weisel Prize for Ethics. Like the father she took care of for many years, Cabrera-Rojas has multiple sclerosis (MS), and she now works with organizations that help MS patients. In her essay, she describes watching the suffering of her terminally ill father, who believes on religious grounds that it is wrong to end one's own life. Cabrera-Rojas reflects that she once shared her father's views, but after witnessing his deterioration, she now believes that the laws against assisted suicide are cruel and unfair. She says that she is worried about what will happen when it is her turn to die of the disease.

Every night, I tuck my father into bed. I cover him first with his favorite flannel plaid bed sheet folded at the chest. I then carefully cover him with two white blankets, the first one folded at the chest and the second one folded at the waist. Once both sheets are in their proper position, I proceed to the next step, his pillow. I must prop it under his head and shoulders and then lift the head of the hospital bed slightly so that he sleeps at an angle and will not choke in his sleep. I then turn off his light, head for my bedroom and turn on the nursery monitor to listen to his every breath until I fall asleep. This is, and has been, my routine for the past three years.

At night, my mind races and demands answers to questions that have no proper response. I find that all of my que-

Yvette Cabrera-Rojas, "Questioning the Arrival at the Station of Departure," Second Prize in the Elie Wiesel Prize in Ethics 2002. Reprinted by permission from The Elie Wiesel Foundation for Humanity.

ries amount to nothing more than the same vicious circle that one is confronted with asking the dreaded question, "Can I find meaning in all of this?" When did I become the parent and he the child? How much pain should a human tolerate? What will tomorrow bring? What is the lesson in all of this? Is there even a lesson to be learned?

Sometimes, I lie in my bed and I try to synchronize my breathing with his. Are we one and the same? It is in this silence that my deepest fear surfaces forcing me to acknowledge that his painful reality could someday be mine because we both have the same illness, Multiple Sclerosis. He was diagnosed in 1981 and I was diagnosed in 1989.

The End Stage of Multiple Sclerosis

My father is 63 years old and everything must be done for him. He must be bathed, fed, clothed, positioned, and everything else in between. My father has what the doctors refer to as "progressive" multiple sclerosis. Progressive, however, is too nice a word; "relentless" is a more appropriate characterization. My father is at the end-stage of this illness. The doctors say you do not die from Multiple Sclerosis; you die from its complications. These words fail to offer any semblance of comfort because death usually does not come silently in the night, as we would wish.

In the book *How We Die* by Sherwin B. Nuland, I read that educating oneself on what is to be expected serves as a defense against the unrepressed thoughts of unwarranted fear and the horror that one is somehow not doing things right. Nuland goes on to state further that each disease is a distinctive process carrying its own kind of "destructive work within a framework of highly specific patterns." He believes that when we familiarize ourselves with the patterns of a particular illness, we disarm our imagination. "Accurate knowledge of how a disease kills serves to free us from unnecessary terrors of what we might be fated to endure when we die." Nuland states that this knowledge will better prepare us to "recognize the stations at which it is appropriate to ask for relief or to begin contemplating whether to end the journey altogether." My father has arrived at that station and is agonizing over what route to pursue.

In the past two months, my father has lost what little movement he possessed below the neck. His fingers no longer move. The muscles in his neck have weakened, affecting his ability to swallow. As a consequence, thin liquids are to be avoided. Foods must be pureed, liquids thickened. He is a silent aspirator. No one can tell if food or drink is entering his lungs. The only telltale sign will be after the fact, when pneumonia and infection set in. My father refuses pureed food, he states that if he is going to die, he will die eating what he likes. He is quick to point out that food is the only remaining joy in his life. What am I to do? What is right? Do I allow him to decide the course of his fate regardless of the inevitable outcome? What is my responsibility as a caregiver?

To compound matters, he has a pressure sore on the outside of his left ankle. Its depth reaches the bone. This is in the process of being treated. Very soon, a pressure ulcer will open on his behind. This one is dangerously located in an area where fecal matter can come into contact with it, risking infection. If that were not enough, he is also presently being treated for a urinary tract infection that is resistant to most antibiotics.

My Father's Religious Belief Forbid Ending His Life

A reasonable person can conclude that my father's quality of life is poor. My father shares this view. Yet his upbringing and religious beliefs render him helpless for he believes that he has no right to request that his life be terminated. Only God can take away what he gives. The Catechism of the Roman Catholic Church states:

Everyone is responsible for his life before God who has
given it to him. It is God who remains the sovereign Master
of life. We are obliged to accept life gratefully and preserve it
for His honor and the salvation of our souls. We are stew-
ards, not owners, of the life God has entrusted to us. It is
not ours to dispose of.

In my opinion, these words serve as nothing more than a
torment to people in my father's condition. And, I resent
them. Those in power usually make policies and laws, and the
meek have no choice but to abide by them. The paradox,
however, in all of this is that we, on the one hand, are told
not to interfere with nature, yet we do it all the time. The
medical community not only interferes with the course of nature, it challenges it! We correct birth defects while babies are
still in vitro. We develop drugs and procedures to combat diseases that, if allowed to follow their natural course, would end
life. It seems that interference can only be tolerated when its
purpose is to prolong life. Who then is the owner of the life
God has entrusted to us?

The Catholic Church states that human suffering can have
a positive value for the terminally ill person and for caregivers. In the "Declaration on Euthanasia" prepared by the Sacred
Congregation for the Doctrine of the Faith, Franjo Cardinal
Seper, Prefect, mentions in his article that "some Christians
prefer to moderate their use of painkillers, in order to accept
voluntarily at least a part of their sufferings and thus associate
themselves in a conscious way with the sufferings of Christ
crucified." Where is compassion? These thoughts serve to alienate the sick and the dying from the living by forcing them
into a life of silence and shame.

Ashamed of his thoughts, my father suffers in this very silence not only the emotional distress that accompanies his
physical condition, but he also agonizes over the indecision to
continue or give in, to treat or to be comforted, to struggle or
to throw in the towel. When will he have his much deserved

tranquility? I often hear people casually comment, "He or she put up a fight to the very end," as if the struggle were a casual experience. I pose the question, what happens to those who choose to recognize that the battle has been lost? Will they be thought of as weak? Will they be viewed as the enemy for reminding the rest of us of our fragility, our mortality? Will it make you sleep better? Can the force to live be so great that it blinds us from the true of meaning of life?

What Will I Do When It Is My Turn to Die?

Lately, my father and I find ourselves debating what constitutes a life of quality. When is enough, enough? I dare not speak for my father. I would do him an injustice to speculate on what he feels or does not feel. I am only a witness to the incredible havoc and destruction that Multiple Sclerosis can wreak on a human. I do not know if I should be thankful for this private tutorial or not. Am I better for it? I cannot answer. Will I know what to do when I arrive at my station? I am not sure. Will anyone assist me in the choice I will make when my turn comes? Probably not.

When I was younger and not privy to suffering, I believed euthanasia was morally wrong. I agreed with the Catechism of the Roman Catholic Church that one does not have the right to dispose of his own life. I now find this statement disdainful. I am not versed in the philosophical works of James Rachels, Thomas More, or Immanuel Kant. I am also too tired to argue the virtues of life or the alphabet of reasons for maintaining it, because at the moment, I am too entrenched in a losing battle with my father to preserve a life, his life; a life that he does not view as useful or rewarding. He has resigned himself to God's will and, as such, will not do anything to willfully interfere with its course, yet he cannot find peace with this decision. My role as his daughter and caregiver is to ensure that his wish be honored, for it is his decision, not mine. I however, am left in ruins to face this same moral dilemma. What will I do when it is my turn? My perception of what is right and virtuous no longer holds true and through my father's agony, I have been humbled. I have been wrestled to the ground and forced to recognize that for the better part of my life I have embraced a lie.

I refuse to believe that *my* life is not in my control. I fully comprehend that I can neither control the actions of others nor the forces of nature. I cannot control the fact that I have Multiple Sclerosis. There was nothing I could do to prevent it. I do not believe that this is some divine test, that it is the cross I was assigned to bear, nor that it is my karma. I do believe, however, that the choices I make on a daily basis, whether good or bad, whether consciously or unconsciously, affect me, as well as the people who surround me, known and unknown. If I am at a point in my life where I am at my most vulnerable, completely dependent and no longer able to act on my own behalf, where *my* life does not meet *my* definition of quality, I would like to know that I have the decision to end my journey, to complete my cycle. The process of dying commences from the moment of birth. It is an integral part of the life cycle. To not embrace death is to not embrace life. I do not fear death; I only fear what I will miss when I leave this world.

Questioning the Law

The ways in which the laws of this country are written do not offer me any solace. What I find is that those who have not suffered or have not witnessed suffering tend to be the most vocal advocates against euthanasia. How can the government stand before me in *Roe vs. Wade* and tell me that I have the absolute right to control my own uterus and take the life of an unborn child, and in the same breath, refuse me the right to end *my* life.

I have to question our government's utilitarian approach that a position is right and a policy appropriate if it produces the greatest amount of good for the greatest number of people. Who determines what is in the common good? Who are these self-righteous guardians? I do not see these guardians in my home when it is time to clean up excrement. Where are they? C.S. Lewis in "The Humanitarian Theory of Punishment" wrote:

> Of all the tyrannies a tyranny sincerely exercised for the good of its victims may be the most oppressive. It may be better to live under robber barons than under omnipotent moral busybodies. The robber baron's cruelty may sometimes sleep, his cupidity may at some point be satiated; but those who torment us for our own good will torment us without end for they do so with the approval of their conscience. They may be more likely to go to Heaven, yet at the same time likelier to make a Hell of earth. Their very kindness stings with intolerable insult...

Is pain and suffering in the common good? Is this not cruel and unusual punishment as stated in the 8th Amendment of the U.S. Constitution? Is this not a conflict? Am I not protected? ...

I Worry About Dying Without Dignity

I worry. If I choose to end *my* life before reaching a particular stage of my illness, my wish should not only be respected, but I should also be able to receive the assistance needed in order to accomplish my goal.

I have given much thought to the following options: (1) I can refuse food and water without the assistance of anyone, (2) I can take my own life before my disease prevents me from doing so, (3) I can wait until it is unbearable, and then request the assistance of a physician to provide me with the means to end my own life, or (4) request that the physician end it for me. I know that the first two options are feasible because I would not require anyone's consent. There would be no need to justify my position. However, after reading much medical literature, dying in the first manner causes more suffering and defeats the purpose. The second option, suicide, does not ensure that it will be done properly. Furthermore, and more importantly, I would have to plan the end of *my* life prematurely for fear that when I am ready to go, I would not be able to complete the task if I were incapacitated. And, if someone were to complete the task for me they would be criminally charged and this is not my intent.

Choices three and four, the most favorable of all options, are not available at present, with the exception of [option three in] the state of Oregon. . . . The law that governs us is the law that forces us to make and live with choices that violate the very core of our beliefs. In the words of Immanuel Kant, "Suicide is not abominable because God forbids it; God forbids it because it is abominable." For me, it is an abomination for someone who is terminally ill or in the end-stage of a disease to be placed in the agonizing position of choosing between emotional and physical suffering and suicide.

Under normal circumstances, free from illness, I would "want to die of death" as Ivan Ilyich so eloquently put it in Leo Tolstoy's novel, *Death of Ivan Ilyich*. But, because this is not my lot in life, I will be left alone to decide my fate, as policies now stand, isolated and deserted by arrogance and ignorance. My request is not to spare myself of any pain in a physical sense; it is to uphold my own sense of dignity. To appease us, the medical community offers palliation, although palliative care does nothing to address this very issue. . . .

I was welcomed into this world with great love and I would like to leave this world the same way; however, because the law, as written, pushes me to clandestinely plot my future demise, an illegal act, my family cannot be present. And, therein lies the tragedy. This dilemma is not unique to me, for all of us will be in this position at some point. The policies that are now in place concerning euthanasia ignore the very principles we strive to uphold in life. The law is in conflict with itself.

I Wish to Be Heard When the Time Comes

My only wish is to be heard when the time comes for me to say that *my* life has been an absolute privilege, but it is now time to let go. So, until that time comes, I will continue to tuck my father into bed every night. I will cover him first with his favorite flannel plaid bed sheet folded at the chest. I will then carefully cover him with two white blankets, the first one folded at the chest and the second one folded at the waist. Once both sheets are in their proper position, I will proceed to the next step, his pillow. I will prop it under his head and shoulders and then lift the head of the hospital bed slightly so that he sleeps at an angle and will not choke in his sleep. I will then turn off his light, head for my bedroom and turn on the nursery monitor to listen to his every breath and, before I fall asleep, I will give some thought to who will take care of me when it is my turn.

Organizations to Contact

Americans for Better Care of the Dying (ABCD)
1700 Diagonal Road, Suite 635, Alexandria, VA 22314
(703) 647-8505 • fax: (703) 837-1233
e-mail: info@abcd-caring.org
Web site: www.abcd-caring.org

ABCD aims to improve end-of-life care by learning which so-cial and political changes will lead to enduring, efficient, and effective programs. It focuses on improved pain management, better financial reimbursement systems, enhanced continuity of care, support for family caregivers, and changes in public policy. Its Web site offers current news, online action guides, and an electronic version of *Handbook for Mortals*, a consumer guide to end-of-life care.

"Care NOT Killing" Alliance
PO Box 56322, London SE1 8XW UK
e-mail: info@carenotkilling.org.uk
Web site: www.carenotkiiling.org.uk

Care NOT Killing is a UK-based alliance of individuals and organizations that brings together human rights groups, healthcare groups, palliative care groups, and faith-based organizations with the aims of promoting more and better palliative care and ensuring that existing laws against euthanasia and assisted suicide are not weakened or repealed. Its Web site contains articles opposing legalization, news, and information about legislation pending in the United Kingdom.

Caring Connections
National Hospice and Palliative Care Organization
1700 Diagonal Road, Suite 625
Alexandria, VA 22314
(703) 837-1500 • fax: (703) 837-1233

e-mail: caringinfo@nhpco.org
Web site: www.caringinfo.org

Caring Connections, a program of the National Hospice and Palliative Care Organization (NHPCO), is a national consumer engagement initiative to improve care at the end of life. Its Web site does not mention euthanasia or physician-assisted suicide; however, it contains detailed information about advance directives and about reasons why provision of artificial nutrition and hydration may increase a patient's suffering.

Citizens United Resisting Euthanasia (CURE)

303 Truman St., Berkeley Springs, WV 25411
(304) 258-5433
e-mail: cureltd@verizon.net
Web site: http://mysite.verizon.net/cureltd/index.html

CURE is a grassroots network of patient advocates from a broad range of professional, political, and religious backgrounds bound together in a common cause: uncompromising opposition to euthanasia and assisted suicide. It also opposes living wills (advance directives that authorize withholding of medical treatment) and, because it rejects the concept of brain death, organ donation. Its Web site contains a number of articles on these topics.

Compassion & Choices

PO Box 101810, Denver, CO 80250-1810
(800) 247-7421 • fax: 303-639-1224
e-mail: info@compassionandchoices.org
Web site: www.compassionandchoices.org

This is the oldest and largest choice-in-dying organization in the nation, created by the unification of Compassion in Dying and End-of-Life Choices, which was the successor to the Hemlock Society. It works for improved care and expanded options at the end of life, advocating comprehensive pain control and palliative care with legal aid in dying if suffering is unbearable. Volunteers in its many local groups provide free counseling and other services to individuals facing terminal illness and their families, as well as to those simply planning for the future. It publishes a monthly magazine and offers recommended publications for sale at its Web site.

Death with Dignity National Center

520 SW 6th Ave., Suite 1030, Portland, OR 97204
(503) 228-4415 • fax: (503) 228-7454
e-mail: use online form
Web site: www.deathwithdignity.org

This non-partisan, non-profit organization has led the legal defense and education of the Oregon Death with Dignity Law and supports those seeking to pass similar laws in other states. Its Web site provides extensive information and links, with emphasis on the needs of student researchers and tips for getting the most from the resources provided.

Dying with Dignity

55 Eglinton Ave. East, Suite 802
Toronto, Ontario M4P 1G8 Canada
(800) 495-6156 • fax: (416) 486-5562
e-mail: info@dyingwithdignity.ca
Web site: www.dyingwithdignity.ca

The mission of this Canadian organization is to improve the quality of dying for all Canadians in accordance with their own wishes, values, and beliefs. It informs and educates individuals about their rights, provides counseling and advocacy services to members, and works to build public support for the legalization of voluntary physician-assisted dying. General information, with emphasis on Canadian issues, can be found at its Web site.

Euthanasia Research and Guidance Organization (ERGO)

24829 Norris Lane, Junction City, OR 97448
(541) 998-1873 (also use for fax)

e-mail: ergo@efn.org

Web sites: wwwfinalexit.org and www.assistedsuicide.org

ERGO is a nonprofit educational corporation established by Derek Humphry, founder of the former Hemlock Society. It is a strong advocate of assisted suicide and/or self-deliverance for people who are suffering from incurable illness. Its Web sites include essays and a blog by Humphry plus information about assisted suicide laws around the world, in addition to offering his books for sale.

Exit International

PO Box 37781, Darwin NT 0821
  Australia
e-mail: use online form
Web site: www.exitinternational.net

Exit International was established by Dr. Philip Nitschke, an Australian doctor who is a strong proponent of legal euthanasia and assisted suicide and who was the first to conduct euthanasia during a short period when it was legal in Australia. It believes that rational elderly people have the right to determine for themselves when and how they will die regardless of their state of health. Its volunteers provide counseling but not assistance with suicide. An e-mail newsletter is sent to members and recent editions are available at its Web site, along with information about Dr. Nitschke and his views.

Final Exit Network

PO Box 965005, Marietta, GA 30066
(800) 524-3948
e-mail: info@finalexitnetwork.org
Web site: www.finalexitnetwork.org

Final Exit Network is an all-volunteer group dedicated to serving people who are suffering from an intolerable condition. These volunteers offer counseling, support, and even guidance in self-deliverance. It is the only organization in America that will help individuals not classed as terminally ill to hasten death. Its Web site contains informational material and detailed statistics from a recent poll about public attitudes toward end-of-life issues.

Growth House
e-mail: info@growthhouse.org
Web site: www.growthhouse.org

Growth House is a gateway to resources for life-threatening illness and end-of-life care. Its primary mission is to improve the quality of compassionate care for people who are dying through public education and global professional collaboration. It is neutral on the issue of euthanasia and assisted suicide. The Web site has extensive information on end-of-life subjects and links to other sites, including blogs, where these subjects are discussed. It also offers online discussion lists for health care professionals.

Hastings Center
21 Malcolm Gordon Rd., Garrison, NY 10524-4125
(845) 424-4040 • fax: (845) 424-4545
e-mail: mail@thehastingscenter.org
Web site: www.thehastingscenter.org

The Hastings Center is an independent, nonpartisan, and nonprofit bioethics research institute that addresses fundamental and emerging questions in health care, biotechnology, and the environment, including those concerning euthanasia and assisted suicide. It publishes a bimonthly journal, *The Hastings Report*, and many other reports and essays, some of which can be viewed at its Web site.

Hospice Patients Alliance (HPA)
4541 Gemini St., PO Box 744, Rockford, MI 49341-0744
(616) 866-9127
e-mail: patientadvocates@hospicepatients.org
www.hospicepatients.org

HPA provides information about hospice services, assists patients, families and caregivers in resolving difficulties they may have with current hospice services, and promotes better quality hospice care throughout the United States. It is opposed to euthanasia and assisted suicide and believes that in many cases hospice patients are being subjected to what amounts to involuntary euthanasia. Its Web site contains many articles about this issue.

**International Task Force on Euthanasia
and Assisted Suicide**
PO Box 760, Steubenville, OH 43952
(740) 282-3810
e-mail: online form
Web site: http://iaetf.org

The International Task Force on Euthanasia and Assisted Suicide is a nonprofit educational and research organization that addresses end-of-life issues from a public policy perspective. It is opposed to euthanasia, assisted suicide, and living wills that give doctors the power to decide when to end treatment. Its Web site offers many articles about these issues, including a detailed FAQ presenting the case against assisted suicide.

Not Dead Yet
7521 Madison St., Forest Park, IL 60130
(708) 209-1500 • fax: (708) 209-1735
e-mail: ndycoleman@aol.com
Web site: www.notdeadyet.org

Not Dead Yet is a national grassroots disability rights organization that opposes physician-assisted suicide. The organization believes that if accepted as public policy, physician-assisted suicide would single out individuals for legalized killing based on their health status and thus endanger disabled people. It also opposes withdrawal of life support from unconscious patients. Its Web site contains detailed material about court cases as well as many other articles.

**Physicians for Compassionate Care
Educational Foundation**
PO Box 6042, Portland, OR 97228-6042

(503) 533-8154 • fax: (503) 533-0429
e-mail: charles.bentz@providence.org
Web site: www.pccef.org

Physicians for Compassionate Care is an Oregon-based association of physicians and other health professionals dedicated to preserving the traditional principle that a physician's primary task is to heal patients and to minimize pain. It promotes compassionate care for severely-ill patients without sanctioning or assisting their suicide. Its Web site contains many articles by members explaining their reasons for opposing Oregon's assisted suicide law and the passage of similar laws elsewhere.

Right to Die Society of Canada
145 Macdonell Ave.
Toronto, Ontario M6R 2A4 Canada
(416) 535-0690 • fax: (416) 530-0243
e-mail: contact-rtd@righttodie.ca
Web site: www.righttodie.ca

This organization lobbies for the legalization of assisted suicide in Canada. It educates the public and presents a complete range of end-of-life options, including self-deliverance, to people who consult it. Its Web site offers articles and back issues of a newsletter.

World Federation of Right to Die Societies
PO Box 570, Mill Valley, CA 94942
(415) 332-18104 (also use for fax)
e-mail: worldfed@pacbell.net
Web site: www.worldrtd.net

This federation of 37 member organizations from 23 countries believes that individuals should have the right to make their own choices as to the manner and timing of their own death. It responds to requests by groups, scholars, and individuals for information about various right-to-die issues. Several times a year, it publishes a newsletter, which is available on its Web site. The site also contains links to articles, news reports, and other right-to-die sites.

Bibliography

Books

Robert M. Baird and Stuart E. Rosenbaum, eds. *Caring for the Dying: Critical Issues at the End of Life.* Amherst, NY: Prometheus, 2003.

Margaret Pabst Battin *Ending Life: Ethics and the Way We Die.* New York: Oxford University Press, 2005.

Nigel Biggar *Aiming to Kill: The Ethics of Suicide and Euthanasia.* Cleveland, OH: Pilgrim Press, 2004.

Robert H. Blank and Janna C. Merrick, eds. *End-of-Life Decision Making: A Cross-National Study.* Cambridge, MA: MIT Press, 2005.

Arthur L. Caplan, James J. McCartney, and Dominic A. Sisti, eds. *The Case of Terri Schiavo: Ethics at the End of Life.* Amherst, NY: Prometheus, 2006.

Raphael Cohen-Almagor *The Right to Die with Dignity: An Argument in Ethics, Medicine, and Law.* New Brunswick, NJ: Rutgers University Press, 2001.

William H. Colby *Long Goodbye: The Deaths of Nancy Cruzan.* Carlsbad, CA: Hay House, 2003.

Ian Dowbiggin *A Concise History of Euthanasia: Life, Death, God, and Medicine.* Lanham, MD: Rowman & Littlefield, 2005.

Ian Dowbiggin — *A Merciful End: The Euthanasia Movement in Modern America.* New York: Oxford University Press, 2003.

Arthur J. Dyck — *Life's Worth: The Case Against Assisted Suicide.* Grand Rapids, MI: Eerdmans, 2002.

Jon Eisenberg — *The Right vs. the Right to Die: Lessons from the Terri Schiavo Case and How to Stop It from Happening Again.* San Francisco: Harper, 2006.

R. E. Ewin — *Reasons and the Fear of Death.* Lanham, MD: Rowman & Littlefield, 2002.

Kathleen Foley and Herbert Hendin, eds. — *The Case Against Assisted Suicide: For the Right to End-of-Life Care.* Baltimore, MD: Johns Hopkins University Press, 2002.

John M. Freeman and Kevin McDonnell — *Tough Decisions: Cases in Medical Ethics.* New York: Oxford University Press, 2001.

Elizabeth Atwood Gailey — *Write to Death: News Framing the Right to Die Conflict from Quinlan's Coma to Kevorkian's Conviction.* Westport, CT: Praeger, 2003.

David C. Gibbs and Bob DeMoss — *Fighting for Dear Life: The Untold Story of Terri Schiavo and What It Means for All of Us.* Minneapolis, MN: Bethany House, 2006.

John Hardwig — *Is There a Duty to Die? and Other Essays in Bioethics.* New York: Rutledge, 2000.

Daniel Hillyard and John Dombrink	*Dying Right: The Death with Dignity Movement.* New York: Routledge, 2001.
Robert C. Horn, ed.	*Who's Right (Whose Right?): Seeking Answers and Dignity in the Debate over the Right to Die.* Sanford, FL: DC Press, 2001.
James M. Humber and Robert F. Almeder, eds.	*Is There a Duty to Die?* Totowa, NJ: Humana Press, 2000.
Derek Humphry	*The Good Euthanasia Guide 2004: Where, What, and Who in Choices in Dying.* Junction City, OR: Norris Lane Press, 2004.
Albert R. Jonsen	Bioethics Beyond the Headlines: *Who Lives? Who Dies? Who Decides?* Lanham, MD: Rowman & Littlefield, 2005.
Leon R. Kass	*Life, Liberty and the Defense of Dignity: The Challenge of Bioethics.* San Francisco: Encounter Books, 2002.
Sharon R. Kaufman	*And a Time to Die: How American Hospitals Shape the End of Life.* New York: Scribner, 2005.
John Keown	*Euthanasia, Ethics and Public Policy: An Argument Against Legalisation.* New York: Cambridge University Press, 2002.

Shai J. Lavi   *The Modern Art of Dying: A History of Euthanasia in the United States.* Princeton, NJ: Princeton University Press, 2005.

Barbara Coombs Lee, ed.   *Compassion in Dying: Stories of Dignity and Choice.* Troutdale, OR: NewSage Press, 2003.

Diana Lynne   *Terri's Story: The Court-Ordered Death of an American Woman.* Nashville, TN: WND Books, 2005.

Roger S. Magnusson   *Angels of Death: Exploring the Euthanasia Underground.* New Haven, CT: Yale University Press, 2002.

Philip Nitschke and Fiona Stewart   *Killing Me Softly: Voluntary Euthanasia and the Road to the Peaceful Pill.* New York: Penguin, 2005.

Suzanne Ost   *An Analytical Study of the Legal, Moral, and Ethical Aspects of the Living Phenomenon of Euthanasia.* Lewiston, NY: Edwin Mellen Press, 2003.

Timothy E. Quill and Margaret P. Battin, eds.   *Physician-Assisted Dying: The Case for Palliative Care and Patient Choice.* Baltimore, MD: Johns Hopkins University Press, 2004.

Philip H. Robinson   *Euthanasia and Assisted Suicide.* South Bend, IN: Linacre Centre, 2004.

Barry Rosenfeld — *Assisted Suicide and the Right to Die: The Interface of Social Science, Public Policy, and Medical Ethics.* Washington, DC: American Psychological Association, 2004.

Michael Schiavo and Michael Hirsh — *Terri: The Truth.* New York: Dutton, 2006.

Mary Schindler, Robert Schindler, and Suzanne Schindler Vitadamo — *A Life That Matters: The Legacy of Terri Schiavo—A Lesson for Us All.* New York: Warner Books, 2006.

Wesley J. Smith — *Culture of Death: The Assault on Medical Ethics in America.* San Francisco: Encounter Books, 2000.

Wesley J. Smith — *Forced Exit: Euthanasia, Assisted Suicide and the New Duty to Die.* San Francisco: Encounter Books, 2006.

Lois Snyder and Arthur L. Caplan — *Assisted Suicide: Finding Common Ground.* Bloomington: Indiana University Press. 2001.

Margaret A. Somerville — *Death Talk: The Case Against Euthanasia and Physician-Assisted Suicide.* Montreal: McGill-Queen's University Press, 2001.

Sue Woodman — *Last Rights: The Struggle over the Right to Die.* Cambridge, MA: Perseus, 2000.

Periodicals

Adrienne Asch
"Recognizing Death While Affirming Life," *Hastings Center Report*, November/December 2005.

Julian Baggini and Madeleine Pym
"End-of-Life: The Humanist View," *Lancet*, October 1, 2005.

Eric Cohen and Leon R. Kass
"Cast Me Not Off in Old Age," *Commentary*, January 2006.

Raphael Cohen-Almagor
"Non-Voluntary and Involuntary Euthanasia in the Netherlands: Dutch Perspectives," *Issues in Law and Medicine*, No. 3, 2003.

Joan Didion
"The Case of Theresa Schiavo," *New York Review of Books*, June 9, 2005.

Elliot N. Dorff
"End-of-Life: Jewish Perspectives," *Lancet*, September 3, 2005.

H. Tristram Engelhardt Jr. and Ana Smith Iltis
"End-of-Life: The Traditional Christian View," *Lancet*, September 17, 2005.

Shirley Firth
"End-of-Life: A Hindu View," *Lancet*, August 20, 2005.

Mary A. Fischer
"To Live or to Die," *Reader's Digest*, May 2003.

Peter Ford
"World Divided on Ethics of Terri Schiavo Case," *Christian Science Monitor*, March 25, 2005.

Faye Girsh
"Ashcroft, Eastwood and Assisted Dying," *Humanist*, May/June 2005.

Nancy Harvey   "Dying Like a Dog," *Human Life Review*, Winter 2005.

Nat Hentoff   "The Legacy of Terri Schiavo for the Nonreligious," *Human Life Review*, Summer 2005.

Jim Holt   "Euthanasia for Babies?" *New York Times Magazine*, July 10, 2005.

Susan Horsburgh, Dietlind Lerner, and Bryce Corbett   "Her Son's Last Wish," *People*, October 13, 2003.

Garret Keizer   "Life Everlasting: The Religious Right and the Right to Die," *Harper's*, February 2005.

Damien Keown   "End-of-Life: The Buddhist View," *Lancet*, September 10, 2005.

Brad Knickerbocker   "Around the Dinner Table, Talk of End-of-Life Care," *Christian Science Monitor*, March 24, 2005.

Frank von Kolfshooten   "Dutch Television Report Stirs Up Euthanasia Controversy," *Lancet*, April 19, 2003.

Daniel E. Lee   "Physician-Assisted Suicide: A Conservative Critique of Intervention," *Hastings Center Report*, January/February 2003.

Hazel Markwell   "End-of-Life: A Catholic View," *Lancet*, September 24, 2005.

Diane Martindale	"A Culture of Death," *Scientific American*, June 2005.
David J. Mayo and Martin Gunderson	"Vitalism Revisited: Vulnerable Populations, Prejudice, and Physician-Assisted Death," *Hastings Center Report*, July/August 2002.
Marc Mazgon-Fernandes	"Death over the Counter," *National Catholic Reporter*, September 23, 2005.
Gilbert Meilaender	"Living Life's End," *First Things*, May 2005.
Sherwin B. Nuland	"The Principle of Hope," *New Republic*, May 27, 2002.
Robert D. Orr and Gilbert Meilaender	"Ethics and Life's Ending: An Exchange," *Current*, October 2004.
Michael Petrou	"A Time to Die," *Maclean's*, September 5, 2005.
Ramesh Ponnuru	"Reasons to Live: The Rational Case against Euthanasia," *National Review*, April 25, 2005.
Andrea E. Richardson	"Death with Dignity: The Ultimate Human Right?" *Humanist*, July/August 2002.
Margot Roosevelt	"Choosing Their Time," *Time*, April 4, 2005.
Abdulaziz Sachedina	"End-of-Life: The Islamic View," *Lancet*, August 27, 2005.

Jeffrey A. Schaler   "Living and Dying the State's Way,"
                      Liberty, August 2003.

Jeff Shannon   "Frankie, Maggie and Me: Inside the
                      Million Dollar Maelstrom." *New Mo-
                      bility*, April 2005.

Wesley J. Smith   "A Duty to Die?" *Human Life Review*,
                      Winter 2004.

Wesley J. Smith   "Dying Cause: Assisted Suicide is
                      Losing Support," *National Review
                      Online*, May 20, 2003.

Wesley J. Smith   "Million Dollar Missed Opportunity:
                      What Clint Eastwood's Oscar-
                      winning Movie Could Have Done,"
                      Weekly Standard, March 1, 2005.

Wesley J. Smith   "Now They Want to Euthanize Chil-
                      dren," *Weekly Standard*, September
                      13, 2004.

Wesley J. Smith   "Why Secular Humanism Is Wrong
                      about Assisted Suicide," *Free Inquiry*,
                      Spring 2003.

Laura Spinney   "Last Rights," *New Scientist*, April 23,
                      2005.

Laura Spinney   "Playing God?" *New Scientist*, Octo-
                      ber 4, 2003.

Thomas S. Szasz   "Kevorkian, Lies, and Suicide," *Ideas
                      on Liberty*, May 2001.

Stuart Taylor Jr.   "What Terri Schiavo's Case Should
                      Teach Us," *National Journal*, April 2,
                      2005.

Carl Wellman	"A Legal Right to Physician-Assisted Suicide Defended," *Social Theory and Practice*, January 2003.
James Q. Wilson	"Killing Terri," *Wall Street Journal*, March 21, 2005.
Barry Yeoman	"Colleen's Choice," *AARP the Magazine*, March/April 2003.

Index